RECYCLED

NURTURE, NATURE, AND FREE WILL IN THE MIND OF AN ADOPTEE

A MEMOIR

JACK F. ROCCO, MD

FIRST EDITION

ISBNs
eBook:
Paperback:

ABOUT THE PUBLISHER

Ingenium Books Publishing Inc. Toronto, Ontario, Canada M6P 1Z2.

All rights reserved.

ingeniumbooks.com

Edited by Amie McCracken

Cover Design by Jessica Bell Designs.

COMING OUT OF THE FOG

There were hundreds of them. On benches, on the ground, snaking along the stairs. Inside, they were lined up down the hallways where they had been waiting for hours, many even since the night before.

They were waiting for us. I still couldn't believe I was part of a team of doctors, nurses, and staff scheduled to see between five hundred and six hundred patients during a single-day outreach clinic at this hospital in Puerto Rico.

It was 1995. This trip was part my six-month rotation at the Philadelphia unit of the Shriner's Hospital for Children. I was in the third year of my orthopedic residency program at Temple University Hospital in Philadelphia, Pennsylvania.

It wasn't just how many people — patients and their families — were crowded and waiting here to see us. It wasn't how many had visible, traumatic, and unusual issues — severe cases of cerebral palsy, scoliosis, clubfoot, and other rare congenital conditions. It was how they were looking at us, as I and the rest of the team walked across the parking lot and up the stairs to the hospital: with admiration and anticipation. And hope. Could I — could we — possibly live up to that? On one hand I was nervous. On the other, I felt blessed, honored, and proud to be part of this highly respected team. It was my first medical experience in the developing world.

As a third-year resident, I was in way over my head with the complexity of cases I was scheduled to see. There was no way to predict or prepare for what type of patient was going to walk, roll, or be carried into my exam room. Fortunately, there were plenty of seasoned physicians close by should I need to consult on a difficult or unusual patient.

Many of their ailments were still unnamed or unique to the particular child. Most of these children had been long-term patients of the hospital, while others were new arrivals from all corners of the island. Their journey often took them several hours or a few days with great difficulty, due to the poverty and limited resources of many of these families. It is not easy to travel with a disabled child even in the best of circumstances.

Once in the clinic, we were all assigned translators, but given the length of the day and the volume of patients, the translators were often pulled in many different directions. We were all expected to have at least a rudimentary ability to speak and understand some basic medical Spanish. Having spent medical school as well as three years of residency in Philadelphia, with its fairly large number of Spanish-speaking patients, I was familiar with the language but certainly not an expert.

During a period when my translator was called away to assist somewhere else, a cute nine-year-old boy walked into my exam room. I couldn't immediately see any obvious orthopedic condition but greeted him with a broad smile and a well-rehearsed "hola." "Hola," he returned. An instant later another cute nine-year-old boy walked into the room, identical to the first. *Twins!* I thought. *That's cool.* "Hola!" I more enthusiastically said to the second child. I looked them both up and down, feeling more insecure as I still could not see anything physically affecting either of them. This was going to be interesting without a translator.

While I was still trying to assess the situation and worrying about my limited Spanish, a third child appeared in the doorway. This child's face was identical to the first two but became the immediate focus of my attention, as it was now obvious that he was the intended target of my expert opinion.

The third boy's face and age clearly marked him as an identical triplet of the first two, but calling him identical would be a gross misinterpretation of the situation. Antonio moved slowly and with great labor as he wobbled into the room with his parents close behind. The widening smile that greeted the first two boys moderated, my eyes flooded with sympathy for Antonio as I more seriously greeted them all with my now-familiar "hola."

His knees were fixed in position and flexed at about a thirty-degree angle. His arms were held at his side with the elbows flexed to ninety degrees and also frozen or severely limited in movement. The muscles of his arms and legs were both dramatically atrophied, and there was a distinct webbing of skin draped over the bend of both his elbows and knees. A diagnosis popped into my mind and I was somewhat excited that I could at least give a name to his condition. Although I had studied the condition in textbooks, this was the first time I had seen and diagnosed a patient with it. This young man had arthrogryposis.

Arthrogryposis is a condition where one or all of the limbs are frozen or limited in motion. The word is from Latin and translates into "wooden joints." There are several hundred different causes of the complex condition, but the effects are similar in that limited joint movement is the result. I assumed it was the result of some genetic anomaly or toxic exposure.

As I examined Antonio's limbs I was trying to put together how this genetically identical triplet could have acquired such severe physical limitations while his siblings were spared. His personality also appeared to be affected: he seemed to be much less outgoing and charismatic than his brothers.

"¿Le pasó algo cuando era más joven?" Did something happen

to him when he was younger, I asked his parents in my halting Spanish.

"Nació así…," they replied. Antonio was born this way.

How could this happen? I thought. I had no idea what could have caused such a dramatic difference among these children. The boys were all genetically identical and likely exposed to the same prenatal environment while in the womb. The three all had the same apparent genetic nature and intrauterine nurture, yet the end result was vastly different for my patient. I was perplexed.

If only I had a pediatric orthopedic textbook somewhere nearby so I could review all the possible causes. Slight variation in circumstance or position can certainly cause dramatic effects in nature. Witness the difference in the height and apparent health of individual stalks of corn in a field adjacent to a busy highway in the middle of August. The grass or corn immediately next to the highway is often smaller, browner, and appears less healthy than the rest of the field. The same type of corn, only a few feet into the field, seems unaffected by the intensity of heat from the pavement. The outer row of corn obviously takes a hit for the rest of the field in protecting its neighbors.

Did Antonio receive less blood flow from his mother and therefore become starved of the necessary nutrients as he developed? Possibly, but he was approximately the same height and weight as his brothers were it not for his frozen limbs. His head and face appeared perfectly normal and identical, so that cause was not my first choice.

Then I thought, *It's awfully crowded in a womb.* So with three hungry growing boys living in such close proximity there must have been quite a battle for space. I could imagine a situation where the other two somehow gained a positional advantage and trapped their unfortunate brother so that it was impossible for him to move. His arms and legs might have been stuck during the stage of development when they should normally have been kicking and punching his mother in the rib cage. His limbs must have been limited or stationary during this period and never properly developed. Intrauterine movement in concert with growth is known to be essential to properly direct or stimulate shape and function of joints. This was the most likely scenario, I decided.

It shouldn't come as a surprise that competition and selfishness is a factor in any human's experience. Sometimes the reason one individual gains the upper hand over another is just chance or dumb luck. It appeared that the two unaffected brothers beat the hell out of their brother and pinned him down before any of them even had the chance to know each other's names.

Were these brothers mean, evil, or predatory against the child with arthrogryposis? Well, not really, but kind of. Their natural code for development (their genetics) was identical, but subtle differences in their position resulted in vastly different nurturing even in the same womb. Was it their free will or subconscious demon functioning in their premature brain that drove them to this unforgivable act? I don't believe they were consciously trying to be mean but they clearly hadn't yet learned the lesson that fairness and goodwill is needed for harmonious cohabitation. Deep down in their early developing brains, while neurons were still interconnecting, they were simply driven by their basic instinct for survival. They were all learning useful and painful realities of the world before they could even breathe its air. Nature, nurture, and free will. They drive so much of our daily existence yet we hardly notice them.

Despite the hero status conferred on us in the faces of the waiting crowd that morning, we couldn't cure or even offer much help to Antonio with the cards he was dealt. All we could practically do was to provide him with braces, crutches, or stretching exercises to improve, but we could never hope to eradicate his problem. We could provide education on the fact that he's not alone in having this condition and ease the parents' fears that they did anything wrong. We couldn't be the superheroes he wanted in his life or reverse the results of his fate, but we could help him to find acceptance and purpose in life. Some feel-good inspiration or motivation certainly wouldn't hurt. The brutal reality was that the best thing we could do for him would be to accept and love him as he was and help him to get along better and, in turn, love himself. This is the part of my job that is often the most difficult. It is infinitely easier to just place someone in a cast until their fracture heals in six to eight weeks.

This case and many others over my career as an orthopedic surgeon have offered me opportunities to ponder these issues of nature, nurture, and free will. I deal with this three-legged stool in one form or other in my professional life on a daily basis. Did my patient get their diabetes genetically from their father's side of the family (nature)? Or was it from the fact that their mother was from the south and served plenty of fried okra with tall glasses of sweet tea over the years (nurture)? Or was it their decision to stop working out after college and slowly gain more than a hundred pounds since graduation (free will)? Often the cause is multi-factorial.

The nature, nurture, or free will questions are more than intellectual exercises for me. They're personal.

As one of millions of infants relinquished by their mothers and put up for adoption, the concepts of nurture, nature and free will have played an integral, intriguing part in my existence. Being a part of the closed adoption system, neither my family nor I were allowed to know the parents from whom I originated.

I was adopted close to the end of what was called the "Baby Scoop Era." Beginning around 1940 and going thru approximately 1970, an estimated four million newborn infants were put up for adoption. The post World War II baby boom era with fast cars, sock hops, no sex education or birth control also lead to a rise in unwanted pregnancies. The mother was often blamed for this lapse in judgment and encouraged to relinquish her child and be "rehabilitated" if she wanted to have any chance to re-assimilate into society. Adoption was presented to most of them as the only option by their parents, doctors, and priests. Just go away to visit an aunt, have the baby, give it up, and come back so no one would know.

Let me make this point strongly and frequently in advance: I had a great family and I have benefited from the upbringing and nurturing they gave me.

There are, however, well-known unintended consequences of this relinquishment and abandonment as an infant. Adopted children are not, in any way, a *tabula rasa*, or blank slate. Everyone involved in an adoption needs to be aware and understand that this *blessing* of a *chosen* child is a unique individual carrying his or her own skills, baggage, and emotions with them. Despite every effort to sugar coat or hide the fact, they have just lost their mother. This is *not* going to go unnoticed. At least not by them.

Similar to Antonio, who was left after birth to suffer the consequences of the things that happened to him in the womb, I've come to realize that I have also been dealing with the aftermath of things that occurred to me in utero.

I think of this as my own version of vanishing twin syndrome. Vanishing twin syndrome was first recognized in 1945 and occurs when a twin disappears during the pregnancy as a result of miscarriage or reabsorption of that fetal tissue.

It's not that I think I had an actual vanishing twin. My "vanishing twin" is more imaginary: the me that never was. The me that I would have been had I been cuddled, nursed, loved and raised by my birth mother in my natural genetic and cultural environment.

I'm not saying that twin would have had it any better or worse. Like it or not, I inevitably have become quite different from that vanished twin in so many ways. How, exactly, is a question that will never be answered. Although my vanishing twin does not exist for real, to this day, the experience that child had of being relinquished by his mother still drives a great deal of my subconscious behavior today.

So who am I? And where did I come from? For the longest time I didn't know and wasn't sure if it even mattered. Thinking deeply about it, I'm not sure any of us fully know who we are. Were my natural tendencies appropriately nurtured in this new family so I could go on to live my best life? They seemed to be, but given that we didn't really know what my nature was, how could we be expected to guess right? Given the adoption system, based in secrecy, shame, guilt, and lies, how could anyone ever expect it to work? Is abortion the answer? I am infinitely grateful that I wasn't aborted and generally had a good experience as an adoptee.

However, I can't ignore the fact that there were significant negative effects on my life as a result of this abandonment.

Adoption is a complex issue and one that is generally poorly represented from the standpoint of the adoptee. Both birth parents — mother and father — are in a difficult situation with tough decisions to make. The adoptive parents are possibly suffering their own issues with not being able to have their own children, so adoption is their second-best option. The organizations that place these children have a daunting task and many pressures associated with their role. A successful placement, any placement, is a victory in their world or a profit in their bank account and neither is inherently the best thing for the child.

As a species, men and women both don't seem to be able to keep it in their pants, whether they be business slacks or yoga pants. We can't seem to stop having children that we really don't want and they keep showing up in orphanages and foster homes around the world. Our public systems have been working on this problem for centuries and have experienced many successes as well as committed horrible mistakes. We really don't understand what effect adoption has on the adoptee. We still don't grasp what takes place in the mind of this child separated from his or her mother, often at birth. My personal experience says that is not insignificant. You wouldn't buy a puppy from an organization that removed the offspring from the mother immediately after birth, but we routinely do it with our own children.

What about this so-called chosen adoptee? They are considered blessed or lucky to have been placed into a good family, and many truly are. Not all placements, however, result in a perfectly harmonious life. Is this child really lucky or blessed? Those are relative terms. It certainly wasn't lucky to be relinquished and separated from your mother at birth. If that happens on the Serengeti plain that infant is doomed! Fortunately, humans seem to be much more compassionate, but how much of that compassion is self-serving? How much awareness does the child truly have of that separation trauma? Research suggests that it's much more than anyone initially anticipated. In 1966, when I was successfully placed in my family, hardly anything was known about this primal wound, or trauma of early parental separation. I was truly both lucky and blessed to have been brought into my family. Many were not.

This book is not necessarily fact for everyone nor obviously the end-all be-all to the argument. This is just my story. The slow realization that comes from discovering the truths around an individual's adoption and the effects it's had on their life is often referred to as "coming out of the fog." From my perspective of personally experiencing it, that's exactly what it has felt like. For me and many other adoptees, there is a lot of fog.

Along the way I have learned a great deal about myself and other adoptees going through the process. I've learned about both my birth and adopted parents and families. I've also learned about genetics, trauma, politics, and race. I've improved my understanding of neural development as well as the importance and role of culture and deception or outright lying. I'm curious about the relatively new field of evolutionary psychology and how behaviors, culture, and social tendencies of ethnicities are possibly inherited, along with physical characteristics, and not just learned. I've mostly learned a great deal about people—all people.

In summary, this is my therapy, my fifty-five-year struggle just trying to figure out me. It's a book which, if considered in full detail, would require several volumes. I'm just trying to tell my story and unfortunately there are many facets. Writing the book has forced me to develop an understanding of how truly complicated human life is. I have come to realize that as a civilized and partially woke society, we should try to give ourselves more credit and love over dealing with this complexity than internal shame or guilt.

I hope you find *Recycled* interesting, entertaining, funny, heartfelt, and informative. As this is my first book, please let me know how I did.

PART ONE
NURTURE

"Nurture your minds with great thoughts. To believe in the heroic makes heroes."

BENJAMIN DISRAELI

CHAPTER 1
RECYCLED

WE WERE CHASING EACH OTHER AROUND THE BACKYARD OF MY grandparents' house when I noticed wasps feasting on some juicy pears that had fallen from the tree onto the grass below. We put on our detective hats to find out where the yellow-and-brown menaces were living.

My father's parents, whom I called Grama and Papa, had a one-story, fourteen-hundred-square-foot ranch-style brick house on the corner of the block that was the center of my universe. Papa, along with other family members, built much of that house in 1954 for his four children: Belinda (Aunt B), Gilda (Aunt Jill), Jack (my father), and Armand (Uncle Armand). On any given Sunday, you could find my ten cousins and me playing stickball in its backyard, riding our big wheel bikes out front, or chasing each other in and out of its three bedrooms. Grama and Papa's lot was a quarter acre, twice the size of any other house on the block, and it always had fresh fruits and gardened vegetables around the perimeter. The center of the yard was cleared for us to run around playing Freeze Tag and Ghost in the Graveyard. One of our favorite activities was climbing the Italian plum trees, white-flowering pear trees, and deep green walnut trees that soared high above the open backyard. Papa planted those trees from walnuts he brought back with him from Rocca Pia, his hometown in southern Italy, which was known as the greenest region in Europe. He felt the trees, grapevines, and garden made his yard feel more like his home country.

"They're coming out of the ground over here," said my cousin Lenny. His two brothers, Timmy and Stevie, were right behind him, peering at the fist-sized hole in the ground. Those brothers were unofficially in charge of entertainment in our group. Their fights back in those days were epic, our reality TV before there was reality TV.

One classic battle royale occurred between the boys during a game of stickball in their parents' backyard. We were using an old aluminum clothes pole as the bat. After a brush back pitch and smack-talking episode, Stevie took off after Timmy, chasing him with the bat. Lenny then quickly took off, trying to stop Stevie from killing his brother. I just sat back and watched the show until, after three or four laps around the yard, we heard the unmistakable slam of the aluminum screen door at the back of the house.

Displeased with the commotion, Aunt Jill, their mother, had burst through the door, letting it slam behind her. She had a wooden spoon in her hand and a desire to control the constant mayhem that was her life with those three boys. Mostly because "they all deserved it." She broke a lot of wooden spoons over the asses, shoulders, and heads of those three. "Jack, you have to go home now." Aunt Jill ordered as she whipped the boys into the house to sit in their room. That's what love looked like in the early 1970s—and she loved those boys a lot.

As the oldest in the group, I took charge of the wasp situation immediately. I was supposed to set a good example. "I've got an idea," I said, as Frank and his brother, Armand, caught up with us by the wasp nest. Frank was generally thin, but Armand was pudgier, so his nickname growing up was Pumpkin. Frank's job was to break as many windows as possible with balls of all shapes and sizes (baseballs, footballs, basketballs, you name it). He was also good for falling in a creek from time to time or splitting open his lip, forcing our parents to make us sit down and stop playing.

Armand's job was to let *us* protect *him*. Around the age of six, he developed Perthe's disease of his hip and walked with crutches and his leg in a sling. Armand and his hip were made fun of a lot. As a result, he felt he had to keep kicking other kids' asses for teasing him. If he got in trouble for kicking their asses, the rest of us got in trouble for not protecting him—and his hip.

"Let's get a bunch of those pears," I told my cousins. "We'll stick them in the hole and trap the wasps inside." Problem solved. Given the size of the hole, it made perfect sense to use them for this makeshift barricade. Apparently, there is a right way and a wrong way to deal with a wasp nest in your backyard. We were about to learn the wrong way.

"Jack, you're going to get stung," said Sharon, who was the older sister to Lenny, Timmy, and Stevie. She was in charge of maintaining the peace with her three brothers. Sharon could put up with her brothers but stopping them from fighting was impossible. As a result of her hopeless job, she suffered like Mary at the cross. Sharon also knew everything that went down but never said anything about it and, as a result, you could always trust her with everything and anything.

"Don't be a jerk," my sister, Lisa, chimed in. "Mom said to stay out of trouble." Lisa was the opposite of Sharon. She could not be trusted with any secrets because she aggressively handled things on her own, even if that meant ratting on everyone. She never apologized for it. If we screwed up, she had to fix it.

"Shut up, Lisa," I told her. "I'm not doing nothing."

The girls stood back as the construction started moving forward. I sent the boys to gather some pears and we started filling in the hole. We began with smaller pears and used sticks to really push them down into this underground fortress.

After we got three or four pears and several stones in place, we looked up to see a swarm beginning to form around our heads. As the buzzing got louder, we realized those worker wasps weren't going to just stand by and let us destroy their home. Within seconds, we were surrounded—so we took off on a forty-yard dash toward the house.

The girls were already inside when we bolted through the back door with such force that our mothers knew we were up to no good.

"I told you!" Lisa shouted. I could always count on her to rub my mistakes all the way in. Then came the barrage of adult questions:

"What the hell is going on?" Papa bellowed.

"Nothing," we said in unison.

"What are you guys doing?" Aunt Jill chimed in.

"Nothing," we repeated.

"Where's Armand?" asked Aunt Lynn. (She was Frank, Armand, and Tami's mother. Tami was still too young at the time to "help" with the nest.)

"He's—" we started. But that one we didn't have an answer for. Apparently, whether you're in the military or a backyard melee, some men do get left behind, and as we looked around Armand was MIA. After what seemed like several very long seconds of confusion, he appeared, crying, in the doorway.

When the wasps went into attack mode, it was every man for himself. Armand tried to keep up with us on his crutches, but, as we soon learned, ended up on the ground taking stings everywhere but his face, which he managed to cover up.

We could never agree on the details: Did Armand trip on his own? Or was he selfishly knocked down by one of us as we bolted for the house? Either way, we certainly remember the red welts that appeared all over his body as a result. With one glance, our hearts sank, and we knew we were all in trouble.

My aunts grabbed their wooden spoons and assumed positions like Samurai warriors from medieval Japan.

"Get over here!" Aunt Jill yelled to her three sons.

"Frank! Why weren't you watching your brother?" Aunt Lynn admonished while winding up to hit her son. Aunt Lynn preferred to whistle while she worked as she whacked Frank a good one on the backside. "Go sit on the couch," she said, and then turned to go after Armand.

"What are you crying about, Armand?" she asked.

"I got stung by the bees," he wailed.

It didn't matter—she was on a roll, and just in case he was lying, he was getting the spoon as well. As she came down with her blow, he quickly thrust one crutch into the air to block it and the spoon splintered into pieces.

"Go sit with your brother," she ordered while bending down to pick up the fragments.

As for me, I never got the wooden spoon. Ever. Even on days when it seemed that I deserved it the most, like this one. One reason was that my mother knew she could wound me much deeper with words. "Jack, you're the oldest. You should know better." Another reason was that, I was the prince. When dinner was served, I sat at the same table as the adults while my cousins sat at a kids' table. I sometimes wondered why that was. I guess it's because I was older and established my seat long before the others arrived. Either way, no one ever challenged my position with the adults, so it just always stayed that way.

A third possible reason I dodged the spoon was my superb acting ability, spurred on by a deep desire for self-preservation. I always gave the appearance of being a good kid around the grown-ups—and was, for the most part. But there were plenty of times when they weren't around and curiosity got the better of me, as in this current situation.

"What happened, Jack?" my mother asked.

"Nothing," I replied. "We were just playing in the back, and there was a wasp nest, and they started coming after us for no reason."

"That's not true," Lisa piped up, throwing me under the bus. Again.

"Go sit with the other boys," my mom directed. No spoon. No yelling. Just telling me to take a seat. She was disappointed and that was worse.

As we were exiled to the living room, Armand was separated from the herd to tend to his wounds.

"Take your shirt off," his mother said. "Where'd they get you?"

"Everywhere!" he cried—and he was right.

"Jesus, they must have got you ten times," Aunt Jill calculated.

When you're raised in an Italian American family in the sixties and seventies, there are certain codes of conduct that you're expected to live up to: Watch out for each other. Don't hit girls. Always stand up for yourself. Doctors and lawyers were way above us and to be respected. The women of the family were the first in our chain of command. Beyond them, it went fathers, Papa, priests, and then God. We heard so many times that "God cries" when we do something wrong. We all sat in silence, realizing how much we had failed in protecting Armand that day and that we had to do better. I understood I was most to blame for having started the whole thing to begin with.

Between the holidays, birthdays, and Sunday dinners, all the grown-ups and kids—twenty-one in total—were constantly at my grandparents' house. It was almost as if we were one family who lived in five different houses. On every special occasion, we'd have big dinners with everyone together. On Christmas Eve, the Catholic Church required we didn't eat meat, so we would have a typical Italian "seven fishes" dinner. Christmas Day was the best meal of the year, with my grandmother's homemade ravioli. Being so close to the lake, we all grew up doing a good deal of fishing. At the end of the summer on Labor Day, we'd have a big fish fry with what we'd caught all year.

On any other day of the week you'd find us dishing out pasta fagioli, linguini with clam sauce, or manicotti stuffed with ricotta cheese. Every meal also came with lots of homemade Italian bread and butter or olive oil to dip it in. The smell of my grandmother's sauce, garlic, and Romano cheese always filled her home with savory Italian aromas. Sure, we ate other cuisines—like the obligatory American fare of meat, vegetables, and potatoes that we suffered through—but we always ended up wondering why we couldn't just have spaghetti.

We got together so frequently that we never went more than a few days without seeing everyone at some point. Often, we would go to my grandparents' house to sit on the porch, just because someone went shopping or church let out or someone had a "fart stuck sideways," which just meant someone had a stomachache. Our close-knit family lived vastly different lives than our neighbors and school friends. They seemed to just do things by themselves, but we had a ready-made group of family, friends, and playmates to spend time with—and we all loved it.

I was born in Erie, Pennsylvania, in late May of 1966. While walking home from kindergarten after school, one of my earliest memories was seeing thick, dark clouds of billowing red and black smoke pouring high into the air from the many steel forges and foundries lining the railroads of that American industrial town.

Nestled up against Lake Erie midway between Cleveland and Buffalo, the city historically played a role in rail and lake travel along this stretch of prime real estate between New York and Ohio. The town became essential during America's quest to seize control of the Great Lakes from the British during the War of 1812. Shipbuilding, railroad, and fishing industries blossomed in the nineteenth century, turning Erie into a boomtown. During prohibition, with easy access to Canada just over the lake, rumrunners transported illegal alcohol into the local speakeasies of the day. The twentieth century and post-World-War-II era established the city as an industrial hub, providing a great deal of work for the waves of young immigrants flooding America's shores. Many families were fed off the backbreaking work performed in this center of American expansion and progress.

"Where are you from?" It was always the first question asked. Like most manufacturing cities, Erie had separate neighborhoods for the Germans, Polish, Irish, and Blacks. My family was Italian, and we were the best. "There are two types of people," my father would say. "Italians and those who wish they were." All these groups lived and worked together, sometimes squabbling, sometimes getting along. In public there was often a common camaraderie of "bustin' balls" with each other any chance they got. Times were good for these blue-collar workers during the sixties and seventies, and the local bars were always packed with many of these dusty men starting at 8 a.m., after the third shift let out.

During those few decades surrounding my birth, there was also unprecedented unrest raging across America. An onslaught of social issues and events led to the assassinations of President John Kennedy and Martin Luther King, Jr. Civil rights battles were raging in the south and many major cities. The Vietnam War left our country and families divided on many fronts. The nation was changing rapidly as old worldviews were clashing with the new ideas of hippies and the sexual revolution, along with women's liberation and racial desegregation.

Class and racial struggles continued into the seventies with no relief in sight. In 1977 lightning struck New York City, leading to a two-day blackout filled with looting and burning of stores. Members of the KKK based in Greensboro, North Carolina, massacred five black individuals in 1979. That same year, Levittown, Pennsylvania, saw over two thousand rioters setting cars ablaze in protest of an oil embargo that led to the price of gasoline skyrocketing.

In Erie, I was largely protected and didn't know anything about all of that. With only three television channels to choose from and a family to shield me from what was going on in the rest of the country, it was as if I lived in a completely different, far more tranquil world. I didn't really know what was happening beyond a two-block radius from my Italian grandparents' house at 1710 West 24th Street.

The Roccos—my family—weren't ever a part of that Italian "godfather" lore of the era. From that standpoint, we weren't like the New York Mafia families you see in the movies. We were more of a Midwestern Italian Lite. There were some smaller Mafia-type organizations in Erie loosely tied to larger families in Cleveland

and Pittsburgh, but that type of crime was never prominent. In the fifties, Erie had a small, somewhat disorganized crime scene, which mostly ran numbers games and small theft jobs. The mayor and several people in his administration were arrested in 1954 and pled guilty to abuse of office for their involvement with a local crime syndicate. The Roccos were all blue-collar working guys, and my grandfather was a long-standing member of the Carpenters' Union. A lot of my family and friends' families worked in the factories.

I was "Little Jack" since my father was "Big Jack," and like any child being brought up in an Italian American family in the sixties, most of my major life choices were made for me. That was totally fine because what was chosen for me was absolutely perfect. I was the first male child in a large extended Italian family and, as the first son, was treated like a prince in almost every way. Of all the kids in the family, I was the favorite. That's my story and I'm sticking to it, for now.

I was especially my Uncle Joe's favorite. He taught me to root for the New York Yankees because we were Italian and that's what we had to do. They had Joe DiMaggio and he was great, so...end of story. We couldn't stand the Boston Red Sox. The Irish kids took up for the Red Sox for some godforsaken reason. I guess they just liked rooting for the underdog back then. Not us. We went with winners—especially if they were Italian. We'd make popcorn, drink Pepsi, and watch the games on Uncle Joe's back porch.

My family was Democrat and John and Bobby Kennedy were a big part of the Democrat affiliation. Even though they weren't Italian—probably Red Sox fans—they were from an immigrant family as well. They fought against discrimination, which united the Irish and the Italians.

And, of course, as Italians we were Roman Catholics. We figured that even though the Romans martyred Jesus, the Vatican was now in Rome. Clearly that meant that Jesus, and therefore God, were also Italian, right? How could we not root for that team as well? It was all for the best because, as you know, God always favors those who look like you, especially those who look exactly like you.

Italian, Catholic, Democrat, and Yankees fans: in my family in the mid-sixties, those were all the best things to be. An added perk was the food. Everyone knew Italian food and the quantities we consumed were second to none. My grandfather led the way as he emigrated from Italy and made us all Americans, the other best thing to be.

Everyone in my family had a role to play that was immediately evident at our dinners. My grandparents had a large, finished basement with a table long enough for everyone to sit at. When everyone poured into the house with excitement, the children would take up playing—or better yet, getting into trouble. The men would take their seats and grab a glass of wine at the table. The women prepared the food like an "army of aunts," which we pronounced "ants" in our Pennsylvania, middle-class accents, led by the general, Gram.

Aunt Lynn was like my mother and Uncle Lenny, Aunt Jill's husband, in that she wasn't Italian at all. That meant she (and they) had to fight harder for their place in the hierarchy and stand up for themselves more often. Aunt Lynn was usually in charge of the green bean casserole because I don't think my grandmother trusted her making Italian food.

Uncle Lenny was Polish, which earned him and his family the moniker "the Skis." Everyone loved Uncle Lenny. He had such an awesome laugh and always told very interesting, intelligent stories. He would often start laughing long before even getting to the punch line. My father and Uncle Armand weren't into that kind of humor, so as he told his stories, they would reply like hecklers in the back of a smoke-filled bar. Uncle Lenny didn't care. His stories cracked him up more than anyone else and that's really the only reason why he told them in the first place.

Aunt B was the oldest of my grandparents' children. She had polio when she was a child and went to the Shriners Hospital for Crippled Children for a year and a half so they could stretch and release her partially paralyzed and contracted legs back to functioning. By the time she left, she could walk by herself without a cane or braces and never wanted any help except when absolutely necessary. My father and Uncle Armand called her "crip" from time to time, which she didn't seem to mind. Their quips were usually met with a strong "Screw you!" but I noticed it did make her try a little harder to not need help. Since it was harder for her to maneuver in the kitchen, she was in charge of espousing her wisdom, whether anyone asked for it or not. Aunt B was a master Yoda for her wisdom and insight into just about everything.

She was lucky. Many kids with polio died back then, but Aunt B eventually got a job, married Uncle Joe, and raised her two beautiful daughters, Julie and Laurie. Despite her polio, she received no favoritism and had to constantly defend herself in this family of eternal ballbusters.

In addition to watching the Yankees, my Uncle Joe loved going to the movies. My first job growing up was to be his uncle sitter. When he was dying of a brain tumor, he still insisted on going to the theater. I would have to go with him to make sure he didn't fall asleep. That wasn't necessarily a bad thing, but he once slept through two or three showings of the same movie! We know this because the manager had to my call Aunt B for someone to come get him. He didn't seem to be in good enough shape to drive.

Uncle Joe apparently also had a temper because that's what brain tumors do. He was sometimes impatient and threw golf clubs when he was playing and had hit a bad shot. I didn't have any problems with him. All I ever saw was his crazy driving. Sometimes as we drove home from one of the western movies he loved, he would drive really fast and go through a few red lights. It was late and no one was on the road anyway, so it didn't really matter.

Then there was one time—after a Saturday matinee—when it was raining so hard the windshield wipers couldn't even move fast enough to clear the view. Well, we got stopped by a train coming through and were about four cars back from the front. His brain tumor must have gotten the better of him and he just couldn't take it any longer. He took off around those four cars and started crossing the tracks anyway. The downpour was so torrential I couldn't even tell you if the train was close or not. My nine-year-old hand gripped the door handle till my knuckles were white and I closed my eyes as we crossed. Fortunately, the train didn't come. We were fine and I never told anyone about this harrowing event.

That was one of the cool things you got to do as prince in my family: be an uncle sitter. It was great, until he died, and that really sucked for everyone, especially Aunt B and his two daughters, Julie and Laurie. I loved him and the stories I have from those brief years I had with him so much.

Aunt Jill was the mother hen of the family. Anytime you did anything dangerous or said something controversial, you would be met with her instant disapproval and a loud "Weeee!" which in Italian apparently meant, "God is crying, and you are probably going to Hell for that one." For Easter, she was in charge of making the baby lamb cake. It didn't really look much like a baby lamb, but this cake was delicious. Aside from the chocolate bunnies, her lamb cake was probably the most important part of Easter. This was especially true because the worst part of Easter was the food. We had ham and no one liked ham. I think it was probably God or the priest or the mayor (who was also Italian, by the way) who made us eat ham on Easter, but Aunt Jill's lamb cake was a great consolation.

My Uncle Armand was the strongman, a five-foot-one former wrestler and truck mechanic who was spunky as hell! He needed to make up for his stature with an inherent toughness he passed on to his children. He was also always good for a laugh, even when that meant putting his body at risk. One evening as we were all playing around my grandparents' house one of the kids threw a plane that got stuck on the roof. Uncle Armand volunteered to go onto the roof to get it. Just to scare the hell out of his parents, he decided it was a good idea to jump off the roof. When the ambulance drivers arrived they didn't suspect it was serious but felt it was best to tie him to the stretcher, just in case. As it turned out, he fractured his spine but fortunately it was nothing serious. For the longest time we just couldn't stop bringing this up any chance we got.

Then there was my dad, who was the go-to guy in the family. He had this Elvis hairstyle with big sideburns and always commanded respect. His love language was doing. If anyone, I mean anyone, needed anything, wanted anything, or he just thought they might need or want it, he would do it for them. He sometimes even let people shoplift from the grocery store where he worked. If they were taking food and looked like they needed it, he'd turn his head and go back to his produce. He didn't talk much and rarely said anything about the favors he did for people. Unfortunately, if he felt they didn't appreciate his work or had somehow screwed him, then they were off the list. Forever! No one wanted to be off the list.

My mother was the perfect balance to my father and the fulcrum upon which our family balanced. Being surrounded by loud, passionate Italian personalities, she never swayed and always kept a calm, level head. She worked tirelessly, and rarely did I ever witness her complain. She *loved* being a mother and was fantastic at it. She was never insulting, always comforting and always there. If she ever caught my sister or me making fun of someone less fortunate than us she would always say something like "Jack, you have to remember that person is someone else's child and they wouldn't want you making fun of them." I witnessed her drinking alcohol one time when I was maybe seven or eight. I didn't like the way it made her seem out of control. I confronted her in front of everyone, cried, and told her she was drunk. She explained to me in private that they were just having fun, but I never saw her drink again after that. I realize now that she deserved to drink more than anyone in the family, but she didn't because of my displeasure.

Gram was the real boss. I referred to her as our keel when I delivered her eulogy years later. The stronger the wind blew to knock us down, the harder she would counter that force in an equal and opposite direction. She was strong but usually did this quietly under the turbulence of the waves. She was always busy, unless she was watching one of her shows. I loved to watch her make gnocchi at the kitchen table. She would make the dough and roll it into a snake before cutting it into little bite-sized portions. She'd then dip her finger in the flour and indent and flip each piece with her middle finger to give it the characteristic ridges and curves. This all happened with such speed and precision, you couldn't help but fall into a trance watching.

Papa was the one everyone looked up to, and he lived up to every expectation as a perfect patriarch. After emigrating from Italy in the 1920s, he worked construction as a carpenter. He retired in the early seventies and much of the time I knew him, he worked in his basement building fine wood grandfather clock cabinets, which he would give to family members, sell cheaply to friends to cover his costs, or raffle off at church.

Papa was a perfectionist in his work, and it was rare to ever see him during the week without a pencil behind his left ear. He had very little formal education but was incredibly intelligent. He had strong, callused hands from his hard days of manual labor but always emphasized education. He taught himself English and took night classes to become a certified carpenter. He loved his Italian heritage but realized the importance of assimilating into the American fabric. He didn't speak Italian in the house unless relatives from out of town came to visit. One of the few times anyone ever saw him cry was when the twin towers came down on September 11, 2001. "Jack, can you believe what they've done to this country?" was all he could say to me.

Technically I wasn't born into the family, I was adopted. As frequently happened in those days, my adoption was closed. Neither my parents nor the birth parents could know each other's identity. My parents explained to me that all they knew was that my parents were two young college students. They couldn't afford to keep a child so they gave me away to a "good family" so I could be raised properly. My sister Lisa had the same story. Our mother and father were now our real mother and father, and that's all we needed to know about that. The nuns told my parents that the father was Italian and the mother was German and Irish. Perfect! My sister's parents were Sicilian.

I didn't really think much about being adopted because no one seemed to have a problem with it. Uncle Joe had been adopted from the same orphanage decades earlier, which may account for the favoritism he paid me. I always knew my story, from before I could remember, and was the one to tell all of my cousins about it growing up. No one seemed to care, we got along fine, and it didn't seem to matter. Still, I do remember thinking from time to time that I looked a little weird compared to the other cousins. In fact, I always looked at myself as a weird kid. I guess everyone is weird at some point, but most of us eventually get over it. Every now and then someone would comment that I looked like my dad or mom, and we'd look at each other and say something like, "Yeah, everyone says that."

Around the age of five, I remember developing a habit of always looking at other people. If I was with my parents and being dragged along on a shopping trip, I would often daydream and wonder if I would ever run into my real parents or an unknown sibling one day. I would especially look at other weird-looking kids. After looking at probably thousands of people over the years, I never ran into anyone who looked as weird as I did, so eventually I stopped. We had plenty to do around the house with the family and I didn't really need to bother myself with looking at other people.

On a trip back to my Papa's house when I was in my late twenties, I began to realize how the years had not only changed the country, but all of us and our little Italian utopia as well. By the 1990s, my family, like many others, was starting to get more complex. The cousins grew up and were maturing, getting married, getting divorced, having children within and outside of marriage. Some of their children, stepchildren, or girlfriends' children were Italian, but many were not. Our Italian identity was being watered down somewhat, especially with the increasing number of children with blended ethnicities and races. I wasn't sure how Papa felt about that.

Papa and I spent a lot of time together over the years in his basement building those cabinets for the grandfather clocks. I credited him with teaching me many of the basic skills of my future career as an orthopedic surgeon by working with my hands at an early age. On that trip in my twenties, we were adjusting the internal mechanisms of a clock that wasn't keeping time. It was a two-man job. One person would turn the hands of the clock for fifteen-minute intervals, allow the clock to chime, and then move to the next quarter. The man in the back would look at the internal workings, adjust the arms striking the chimes as needed, and try to figure out the problem.

"You know, Jack," Papa said to me. "I think we almost have more recycled kids in the family now than we have our own."

"I know, Papa," I replied. "What are you gonna do?"

I'd never heard that term "recycled kids" before and I'm sure someone would probably find it offensive. He didn't mean it in a derogatory way. It was just the way his Italian mind reformulated American words and concepts into what he wanted to say. He loved every one of those "recycled kids" as his own. I never heard him degrade any ethnic group. He had suffered through his own discrimination as a young immigrant who spoke poorly. He was well aware of the cultural changes the country—and our family— were going through and seemed to accept it. He'd seen this before. It happened when he came to America and when the Irish came before him. He didn't always agree with what was going on, but always had some wisdom to impart.

I had mostly forgotten by that point that I was adopted. At least I didn't mention it as much. I'd stopped thinking I was weird, but as with many of the repeating cycles in the natural universe, I think I'm back to being weird again. Perhaps I just settled back into my original weird self. Or maybe it wasn't weird, just different. It's funny how things changed once I looked at my life through a different set of eyes.

It wasn't until years later, when my grandfather passed away and I was writing his eulogy, that I thought back to this workshop conversation. *Holy shit!* I thought. *I was recycled, too.* I realized for the first time that I was the original recycled kid. There was no question that I had earned my Rocco stripes by then. My assimilation into this wonderful cast of characters was so complete I sometimes wondered if they were lying to me about the adoption. I never thought I was ever anything other than a proud, full-fledged, somewhat spoiled member of the family. I was, in fact, recycled, but it didn't seem to matter one bit.

CHAPTER 2
GETTING DOCTORED

STRONG VINCENT HIGH SCHOOL WAS AN OMINOUS SIGHT ON MY FIRST day of ninth grade, with its large concrete pillars, aging façade, and its reputation as a tough school.

"The seniors are going to pick on you," I was told. I had heard we — me and my cousins — might even be egged or doused in shaving cream when we started at SV in the fall of 1980. We had heard the stories of race riots from six to eight years earlier, when my cousins Julie and Laurie were students there. One of their friends allegedly had to jump out of a window to escape one such riot in the early seventies. They seemed like adults to the rest of us. They hung out and smoked with a wacky group of friends, and they babysat us on the rare occasions our parents would go out. Like to the Italian Dance.

The Italian Dance was a major event every year, sponsored by the Rocca Pia Society, and held at St. Paul's Church. We'd get to have sleepovers, and eat Italian subs and pizza from Damore's on 26th Street. We rarely ate restaurant food. "Why do you want to spend all that money when you can make it better yourself at home?" my father would remind us. But we enjoyed the change, especially hanging out with our older cousins and their hippie friends, who seemed different enough from us they might as well have been from another planet.

The flailing economy of the seventies was about to improve. We were still in the middle of the Iranian hostage crisis that fall. The country seemed much more united in its resolve to tie as many yellow ribbons as possible around the old oak trees in the city than it was at the start of the race riots. By January of my freshman year, Ronald Reagan was in office and the hostages had been released after 444 days. My parents liked Jimmy Carter, especially for his recommendation to wear sweaters in the house to conserve energy. "See! Jimmy Carter agrees with me," my father would say as if he was in the president's Cabinet. We'd been wearing sweaters and wrapping ourselves in blankets in the house years before Carter called upon the country to do the same. My father felt like Nostradamus over this foresight and frugality for his country.

Fortunately, none of the threats materialized for me at SV, and my experience at high school was great. Many of my friends from middle school had continued on to SV, too. Everyone was lower- to middle-class and came from various ethnicities. I played football and ran track and therefore hung out with most of the cool jock kids. I always got good grades, was in the gifted program, and was able to take a number of advanced placement classes for college credit as well. The only AP class I didn't take was history. Why would I? That stuff had already happened and I was looking to the future. As an adoptee, I didn't really have a past, so it never seemed to concern me.

My classmates Jimmy, John, Greg, and Robbie liked that I wasn't afraid to help them out during test time. We developed a system of hand signals and gestures so I could share my answers with them. This continued even after the teachers suspected something was up and moved me across the room away from everyone. We were really good at it and never got caught.

It turns out, despite only being about five-foot-eight, I had a little speed as well and was able to letter in both football and track all four years. By my senior year, I was a starter on both offense and defense as a halfback and cornerback, respectively. Football was my favorite sport, but I used track as a way to stay in shape and work on my speed. Usually, the white guys did the distance runs and the Black guys sprinted. I was a sprinter. The sprinters weren't uptight like the distance runners and liked to have fun. They were also the stars on the football team, and we got along great.

On the 4x400 relay team, I was the only white guy along with three Black classmates. They called me "Lickety Split" after the white main character in the 1979 TV movie *The Jericho Mile*. I thought it was cool to be the only white guy on the team.

We ran every day and taught ourselves baton passes because we really didn't have a coach. Our coach was basically an alcoholic and made a few thousand dollars to coach but rarely came to practice. Despite this lack of supervision, we never had any problems and certainly never thought about race riots. Unless we lightly joked about my nickname, we rarely even mentioned race. When we were racing against the private all-boys school, Cathedral Prep, and saw their four white runners, I'd say something like "Hey, I'm going over there to stand with those guys" and start moving in that direction. "Shut up!" my teammates would shout back at me. "Get back here!" They knew where I belonged, and so did I.

Probably because of my diverse interests and friends, I eventually became senior class president and was voted most likely to succeed. I graduated in the top ten of my class and felt well prepared for my college years. Mrs. Mastrian, my AP biology teacher, was the first teacher I ever mentioned the possibility of becoming a doctor to when she asked me what I wanted to do. She said she thought I had the intelligence for it, if I could handle the stress and pressure of the medical field. "Papa, I think I want to be a doctor," making my grandfather the first one in my family I told. We didn't know there were many different types of doctors, but he knew what I meant. "Jack, you're smart, you can do whatever you want," he said.

For those of us at Strong Vincent, the University of Pittsburgh was considered a top-tier school. It was either Pitt or Penn State for the top students, and I chose Pitt. A classmate told me Pitt had a medical school, and if I wanted to be a doctor, it was better to go there. Solely on this advice, I applied to only one school, never visited, and was accepted without a problem. I became the first in my family to go to college and they were uncertain how to help me with that decision.

"Jack, you always make good decisions," my mother would say.

"What the hell do I know?" my father asked. "I barely made it through high school."

My parents moved me down to Pitt, about two hours south of Erie. My mother says she never cried so hard as when she saw me walking away from the car toward my dorm room with that wicker basket full of Papa's pears in my hands. I couldn't wait to get started. Pitt was far enough away that I could be on my own but not so far that I couldn't hitch a ride home with any of a number of other classmates who were also from Erie.

Most of those Pitt classmates were from Cathedral Prep. We made fun of them in high school and were always a little intimidated by their seemingly higher wealth and greater privilege. "HO-MO-SEXUALS, HO-MO-SEXUALS," we'd chant during every game against them. They usually beat the hell out of us on the field but I guess since they were an all-boys school, that was all we could think of to get back at them. We tried to mix it up a little once when we all yelled in unison, "Hey, Prep! Where's your girls?" They quickly retorted with, "Hey, SV! Where's your basketball team?" So that sort of backfired. It turns out that once I actually met these guys and got to know them at Pitt, we all became really great friends. We frequently laughed our asses off over those games and ridiculous chants. See what happens when you leave Erie? Turns out there's a whole other world out there and it ain't all that bad.

Of course, I was scared of starting college, but I truly looked forward to getting settled and seeing what I could do. I decided to major in behavioral neuroscience — a perfect blend of biology, chemistry, and psychology. I thought it would allow me to prepare for medical school but also give me something to fall back on if that didn't work out as planned. It was a relatively new field and I loved the genetics, neurotransmitters, axons, receptors, addiction, and pathology resulting from various chemical imbalances or anatomic abnormalities. It was a tough major. But I wasn't in college to party; I was there to learn.

I had some early struggles with classes but eventually got into a groove. Then in the second semester of freshman year, chemistry nearly ruined me. I started off by going to every class, taking copious notes, and thinking I understood the subject. The thing I began to focus on most in class was the fact that the professor seemed to wear the same shirt and pants every day. I wondered if it was *actually* the same shirt and pants or if he just had a closet full of yellow button-downs and khaki pants.

The first test came and reared its ugly head. The professor gave me a D. What the hell? I nearly jumped off one of Pittsburgh's many bridges over that. I had never come close to even a low B in high school. I couldn't understand what had happened. That test was nothing like the professor's lectures. I quickly understood: he was testing on the book but his lectures were just filler information. I had read through the book some but figured whatever he was lecturing us on was more important. Some college professors were more interested in doing research than teaching a large class of freshmen. Maybe teaching just wasn't his thing.

Before the second test, I still went to class and took more notes but started to follow along more with the book. The second test came and I anxiously awaited my results with optimism...C+. Ugggghh! I thought it was this guy's job to teach us what we needed to learn. I realized then that this was one of those "weed-out classes." It was his job to fail us. I started to wonder if they didn't pick him on purpose. They probably also told him to wear the same clothes every day just to further screw with us. I had to get this bullshit down, and fast.

At this point, as the first college student in the Rocco clan, I was a little bit of a golden child and wasn't interested in going back to Erie with my tail between my legs. No one chooses who we are or where we come from, but we do have control over where we're going. I couldn't fuck this up. The final exam was my last chance to pull this off and, fortunately, it was worth a higher percentage of my final grade.

I stopped going to class completely, as I realized it was a total waste of time. Instead, I went to the library during my scheduled class time, as well as early every morning and late into the night. I started back at the beginning of the book and had to try and teach myself the subject. The final came and I freaking nailed it. I got the sixth highest grade in the class, out of 350 students. My score totally blew away the average and secured me a B+ for the course. Thank God — and take that, you every-day same-shirt-wearing, poor excuse for a college professor! Weed someone else out.

The first thing I learned from that class was that I couldn't rely on anyone else. If I wanted something to happen, I had to make it happen. Like when my Aunt B found herself being called "crip" and working to ensure she didn't need to ask for help, I found something inside myself that was pushing me to go beyond my own and other people's expectations. I found my reason — my why. The second thing I learned was not to focus on stupid shit. My chemistry professor was the smart one for not wasting time picking out clothes. I was the moron for worrying about it. There was a fire burning deep in my soul that I didn't want to disappoint my family. No nerdy chemistry professor was going to extinguish that. No other class was going to give me that much anguish again, ever. I found the key, and it was inside me, but it wasn't easy to find and bring it out.

Okay, I'll admit it now: I eventually did learn to party, but only after my studying was done. During my freshman year, I joined the Beta Theta Chapter of Sigma Chi. My parents had nothing to add on this decision either. I was invited to a party, I met some guys, they asked me to join, and I wanted to, simple as that.

"But Jack, those fraternities haze those kids and don't you have to go through 'Hell Week'?" my mother worriedly asked me.

"Ma, they don't do that anymore. That was the past," I assured her. I wasn't really sure, but ended up being kind of right. We did get a little hazed but fortunately it was all in good fun and nothing dangerous or too demeaning.

Joining the fraternity ended up being one of the best things I could have done. I was quickly accepted and moved up the ranks in leadership roles, becoming vice president as a sophomore, treasurer as a junior, and president by my senior year. We had a lot of fun, but I also learned a great deal about managing people, leadership, and partisan politics. My friends Staud and Tommy were great at teaching me my leadership roles well. There were always members of the fraternity who wanted to just buy more beer, but the responsible ones knew we had to allocate some money for capital expenditures, like a new stereo system or an industrial kitchen. It certainly wasn't Congress, but the topics were just as polarizing and the bickering was similar. I also played intramural sports—and learned to balance my interests while continuing to get good grades.

I was starting to recognize that there was something very different about me. I sensed that my family was a very strong motivator for me but no one in my family had any direct influence on my college career and as none of them had been to college they had no insights to share. They let me be. Despite finding myself in a new environment, I was able to adapt to a certain degree.

Adoptee circles talk about the importance of genetic mirrors in their life. Under a normal family situation the child is constantly looking at their parents and their parents are looking at them. There is genetic familiarity. The child looks or acts like the father or mother. They know what their skills are likely to be and some of the negative traits that may have been passed along. There is a self-fulfilling feedback loop that both parent and child seem to follow to nurture or modify certain behaviors to their liking.

My parents and I didn't have that, per se. Like many other

adoptive parents and adoptees, my path was taking me in a completely different direction. I didn't really look like them and didn't always act like them but it was okay. "Let's see where this gets us," was the underlying theme.

A girl I dated during college once told me what an older fraternity brother said about me, which always stuck. His name was Ed and he said that he really liked me because "Jack can be so good and so bad at almost the same time." I thought about that a lot but never really understood. He meant it as a compliment, but I always saw myself as good and was a little offended that he thought I was bad in any way. I really looked up to him. I didn't really judge people and I tried to be friendly with everyone.

As a child I was always searching through crowds for familiar-looking faces. What I was probably doing was looking for mirrors of some sort. I was looking for me. I was constantly scanning the crowd for people I could mimic or bond with who were similar to me. I didn't necessarily see me in my family but those similar people had to be out there somewhere. Some of those I met were "good" and some were "bad." I looked at them all, trying to see where I fit. I didn't necessarily rule anyone out until I figured it out or they burned me.

Ed talked me into wrestling for the fraternity. My fraternity was well known for wrestling and won the fraternity intramural tournament every year. I had never wrestled but when he first met me, he grabbed me by the bicep and asked, "Do you wrestle?" I said no, and he quickly replied, "No problem, I'll teach you." That was it. I was now a wrestler.

For the next several years he worked with me on the basics. On multiple occasions, he would just randomly attack me from behind —no matter where we were. If it was during a party, he'd proceed to rub my face into the beer-soaked floor till I started fighting back. Eventually I got better. By my junior year, I won my weight class, which was no easy task in Pittsburgh. Pennsylvania is a wrestling state, and all the wrestlers I was going against had wrestled since high school or earlier.

Ed—along with Knox, Slow, Goad, and Paulie—took an interest in teaching and working with me. I didn't want to let them down. I worked my ass off learning how to wrestle, and got into very good shape before the tournament every year. I even brought my weight down from 165 to 150 pounds to fill a vacant slot we had on the team. I always attributed it to my blue-collar, hardworking mindset, but I think it was something more, something deeper. I wonder even today if it was from some desire to not only fit in, but to truly belong despite my uncertainties. I always worked harder than others, regardless of what it was. Maybe it was something I'd inherited from my mysterious birth parents. I had no idea what it was, but there was something unusual about my drive. Despite my fantastic upbringing, something didn't quite add up.

My academic life continued. I took the MCATs, applied and interviewed at a number of medical schools, and was accepted to Temple University School of Medicine in Philadelphia. I was horrified. That's right: not delighted or excited, as I should have been, but shocked and full of fear. *Are you shitting me?* I thought to myself when the letter came in the mail. I would've been happy if I wasn't so scared out of my mind. Me, the son of a working-class dad and a homemaker mom, was on his way to having MD after his name? None of it seemed real, but I'd asked for it and now it was happening. *How in the hell am I going to pay for this?* Buckle up, big boy; we'll see if you can handle the stress that Mrs. Mastrian wondered if you were up for.

The night before my first day of medical school, I remember ironing a button-down dress shirt and dress pants to wear. In college, if we had a formal event, I would fold my pants ever so neatly and lay them on the back of my roommate Sparky's beach chair in our Sigma Chi bedroom. (Eventually we all decided he needed to change his name to Spike to sound tougher.) I'd then put a towel over the pants and rest my back on them as I studied. After a while I would flip the pants over and continue reading. In no time at all, I got some studying done, the pants looked reasonably wrinkle-free, and I'd killed two birds with one stone. I had to be better than that for the first day of medical school, so I ironed. I was that petrified!

On the first day of medical school, everyone in my class seemed to be from the right side of the tracks. I was from much closer to the tracks — literally. I grew up about four blocks from the tracks and Erie's industrial complex. We could usually hear the trains and factory sounds most hours of the day. Many of my classmates had parents who were doctors, lawyers, and neurosurgeons. Other than my pediatrician, I had never met a doctor, and certainly never outside of the office. I couldn't imagine that some students actually lived with one or even two physicians.

My parents and family supported me emotionally, but financially, that just wasn't an option. I drove a bright yellow 1981 Chevy Chevette that I got real cheap from my Aunt Joan, my mother's sister, and Uncle Benny. Some of the other kids drove BMWs. I was just getting deeper and deeper in debt, with loans that got so high in a semester they easily surpassed what my parents paid for their house. It didn't seem like a real amount of money I'd ever be able to pay off.

Once again, I had been dropped into a completely new circle and was surrounded by people I had little experience relating to. I had served people of this class as a busboy and waiter in high school but was never on the same side of the fence. My classmates weren't really *that* bad, but socializing with them sometimes made me feel like I was sneaking into a country club. Many of my classmates would go away to the beach or Cancun with or without their parents for spring break. I went home to Erie. One time I literally had to stop at several streams as I drove across the Pennsylvania Turnpike to collect water to put into my girlfriend Bonnie's overheating car. In this group, I had to try to once again be a chameleon: stay aloof, never let them get a straight shot at my core. Glancing blows I could handle, but I had to avoid any direct hits. Bonnie was the first person close enough for long enough in different situations with me to realize the prominence of this blending skill.

"No matter who you're with you automatically change to fit in with them" she mentioned.

"You're crazy! Everyone does that." I assured her.

"No, not like you." I knew for sure she was crazy.

Temple actually had a fairly good number of diverse students enrolled. As I got to know the other students, one thing I noticed was that pretty much everyone in my class had a really interesting story. One classmate played for the New York Giants as a scab during the NFL strike a few years earlier. One was an Olympic athlete on the Haitian team. One was even a former nurse who was now divorced, raising kids, and had gone back to medical school to give them a better life. She complained that while us "young kids" without responsibilities were out drinking beer and eating cheesesteaks, she was home doing laundry and ironing every weekend—and not just the night before the first day of class. I couldn't imagine.

A few of my classmates had come to America on refugee ships from Vietnam or Cambodia. One close friend and classmate was an African-American who grew up in a rough neighborhood in New Jersey. He wanted to be a family doctor and return back home and serve his community. I had my story of being an adopted, blue-collar, Italian immigrant kid and went with that. These were people out to change the world, and I wanted to be a part of that!

Turns out, I did just fine. It wasn't easy, but once I made it past the first few traumatic weeks with that deer-in-the-headlights look, I snapped out of my funk. There were a couple Erie guys from Prep in my class who made the transition much easier. Chris, Dan, and Paul were scared to death too, so I didn't feel so bad. I was still the public-school kid and they were private-school guys, but now we were all the same. We were all doctor wannabes from "Dreary Erie, the Mistake on the Lake," and we owned it. We carpooled together often, singing the B-52's song "Rock Lobster" a cappella on our morning commute. That became our theme song for no particular reason other than it fired us up before class.

We all soon realized that while we weren't the most intelligent students in the class, we weren't the least either. Neither intelligence nor wealth could protect any of us from fear, though. We were all terrified in our own way.

It became obvious that you don't get into medical school simply by being smart. We also had to have the *chutzpah* to somehow convince ourselves that we were smarter than everyone else. There was way too much to learn and we were going to be humbled, but had to become immune to it. It was like an egotistical staring match. We needed to fool our colleagues and ourselves into believing we were more than we thought. Eventually we would become better yet realize we might never quite get to where we convinced ourselves we'd be, or perhaps we'd exceed it. It was okay, and it was all a process. Just fake it till you make it. I was good at that.

The first two years of medical school weren't as difficult as that freshman chemistry class in terms of complexity. Volume was the problem. I often felt like a dog trying to take a sip out of a fire hydrant. It seemed as if more information spewed onto the pavement than I could ever get into my mouth. The volume of material that was thrown at us on any given day was immense. It was difficult for me to focus while sitting in the same auditorium with two hundred other students for up to eight hours every day. It was numbingly painful. The distractions in class were ridiculous and brown-nosing and one-upmanship was a constant annoyance. Other people spent so much time and energy being anxious about everything. That wasn't moving anyone closer to his or her goal and just made me more nervous as well.

I did not want to be like many of them so I isolated myself. At some point, I resorted to my old chemistry class strategy and stopped attending class altogether. I actively tried to avoid all of that intra-class drama. *Just go to the library and do the work*, I thought. I promptly awoke at 7 a.m. and went to the library to read or study till noon. I'd often grab a cheesesteak or grocery shop and make myself a sandwich while I watched an episode or two of

Hogan's Heroes. After working out in my apartment basement, I'd head back to the library.

I ate a lot of meals alone, but wouldn't describe myself as a loner. I went out and was social as well. I still had a lot of great times with my classmates. I think I was fairly well liked, but there was work and there was socializing, and I tried to keep the two separate. I wasn't trying to be class president this time. I seriously just had to survive.

The second two years were clinical, where we rotated around to all the specialties. We worked in internal medicine, surgery, pediatrics, ob-gyn, psychiatry, family practice, and some electives here and there. We were up early, making rounds, presenting to residents and attendings, and taking night calls. With supervision, I interviewed patients, delivered babies, assisted in surgery, and put in central lines and chest tubes. By my senior year, I eventually got to do a trans metatarsal amputation of a diabetic foot by myself. The female surgeon I was working with just watched. "Surgery is like sex," she told me. "It's fun to watch but much better to participate in. You'll do this one."

We even got our own beepers. I couldn't stop checking that beeper just to make sure I didn't miss a page. I couldn't decide whether it should be on my left or right hip so I could efficiently get to it quick enough. Every time it went off was like a hit of heroin for me. That familiar beep let me know someone needed me and I had to answer it as fast as I could.

The first time I heard my name called over the loudspeaker by the page operator was an even bigger deal. That was like being called up to receive my Oscar. "Dr. Rocco, paging Dr. Rocco 3579. Dr. Rocco 3579. Best actor, Dr. Rocco." It was great! Thirty years later, just like a heroin addict, that beeper habit of mine has only gotten worse. Now, no amount of beeping or texting is ever enough to give me even the slightest rise in my pants. I hate it.

Once again, I somehow worked hard, spun my magic, had all the right moves, and matched for one of only four spots in Temple's orthopedic surgery program. I learned that the other three doctors with whom I'd be working were an orthopedic surgeon's son, an internal medicine doctor's son, and a lawyer's son. *I got this.*

My whole family was planning to come to Philadelphia to attend my graduation. Aunt Jill and Uncle Lenny hadn't been out of Erie for twenty-five years by that point. This was a big deal. Papa called me the morning of the trip and said he couldn't make it. He was having anxiety and had a bad heart and just couldn't get himself to travel. I was crushed and seriously teary-eyed.

I tried to slowly talk him off the ledge and explain how important it was to me to have him there. I told him to go get a Valium out of his cabinet, take it, and just sit in his chair for a few minutes. He was truly sorry but didn't expect that was going to work this time.

About a half hour later, my mother called and said he was packing up the car and bringing a little handheld battery-operated fan so he could breathe. He wondered if I wanted him to bring me some of his dried Italian sausage before he left. Of course, I did!

That trip was like a *Beverly Hillbillies* episode titled, "The Roccos Visit Philadelphia." I took my family all around the city showing them the Liberty Bell, Valley Forge, and Little Italy, where Rocky ran through the market with all its meats, vegetables, and burning barrels on the street corner. Papa loved it all and I have a great photo of him straddling a cannon at Valley Forge. This little Italian guy looked like George Washington with this large phallus between his legs, about to kick some serious redcoat ass. He loved this country.

I thought they were all going to love Little Italy, but my grandmother was afraid.

"I know it's nice, Jack, but too many people," she told me. "Let's just go back to the hotel and eat at Denny's tonight. I love their mashed potatoes."

Oh well, the general had spoken: Denny's it was. She even had them make her a special order of mashed potatoes one morning for breakfast. That Denny's was way better than the Liberty Bell to her.

In the few weeks before residency, I wish I could tell you that I finally relaxed and believed *I got this*. That would be a lie. I didn't think I "had this" at all. I was terrified but wasn't going to let anyone hear my true thoughts.

This time, it wasn't just the question of worthiness that created an emotional tug-of-war inside of me; it was also whether I was letting go of my past. I was aware of wanting to move upward in my life but simultaneously not wanting to abandon the family and modest upbringing I loved so much. I wanted to make my family proud and was hungry to prove to myself and everyone else that I could actually do it. Unfortunately, I also seriously questioned whether I'd made the right choice by leaving the comforts of 1710 West 24th Street behind.

Here's another thing: becoming a doctor is great. Everyone is so proud of your accomplishments and puts you on a pedestal every time you get a new piece of paper to hang on your wall. You are their hope. You are going to change this very complicated system that is thirsting for someone, anyone, to make it better, like it should be. It should be cleaner and more comfortable and not so damn expensive. Despite the system's every effort, it still eventually leads to death for practically everyone we know. Thank God I was going to be the one to finally change all of that.

Well… then you become a doctor and suddenly, almost as soon as you finish taking the Hippocratic Oath, all those problems are miraculously your fault. "Why is it that you doctors charge so much money?" "Jack, why do we have to wear those gowns with our ass hanging out when you are just listening to the lungs?" "My mother went to the doctor for a simple check-up and they ended up doing a CAT scan on her liver. Turns out they found she has only one kidney and now she needs to go through other tests. Now why is that?" It never ends for the rest of your life.

The toughest question I was ever asked came from one of the women who worked the cafeteria line at Temple. It was a Friday during lunch and, for whatever reason, it was slow enough that I actually had time to stand in line and pay for a meal. We had voucher cards, which helped pay for our meals when we were on call, so we rarely actually paid. Nonetheless, we still had to go through the line to ring up the charges.

The lines were long and snaking between each other so that everyone was shoulder-to-shoulder, and the place was bustling with noise. As she rang up my total, the cashier, Saundra, looked me in the eyes and with absolute sincerity and a complete lack of embarrassment, asked, "Dr. Rocco, I got a condom stuck up inside me. Is it gonna come out?" There was a really long pause as I looked back and forth between her, my tray, and the ten people behind me in line. I think I said something like, "Uhhhh." How you like those brains? Where do I even begin with that? Well, finally, I was a doctor. Hide the nurses and let the party begin!

CHAPTER 3
SUPER MEN AND
WONDER WOMEN

EVEN THOUGH I STILL HAD A GOOD DEAL OF SELF-DOUBT, I WAS becoming more confident in my own natural tendencies and always seemed to choose the more difficult path, I was feeling more comfortable being uncomfortable. I almost preferred it. If I relaxed, it was just an opportunity for someone to sneak up behind and snag me. My best defense was to keep running. I felt fortunate to have matched to the residency program at Temple, mostly because I knew it wasn't going to be easy.

Temple University Hospital is located in North Philadelphia and is directly across the street from the medical school. During my first two years of medical school, every day we looked with admiration at this shiny twelve-story palace, eager for the day when we would enter its halls. When the weather allowed, we would sit outside and just stare at it while eating our lunches from one of the many food trucks selling cheap street meat to us budding young physicians. This building was our beacon of light. It was our siren in the dark, tempting and challenging us to cross that street in our quest to become real doctors — medical professionals who are often an under-appreciated band of superheroes. I knew it was going to be an honor to work in this field and my time at Temple was my first chance to witness firsthand the daily effort of these talented individuals who are all a part of a complex global structure.

During my interview for medical school, a second-year student who gave the tour mentioned that it was a great place to train because you got to see and do practically everything there.

In the eighties and nineties, we had plenty of great professors teaching us our trade, but also had a tremendous amount of autonomy. Across the street, the residents ran a good deal of the show. Those residents often looked like gods to us, and I was afforded the opportunity to be one of them. There was always a great deal of patient care for the residents to participate in and perform as many procedures as they could handle very early in their career. That meant more learning, which was the currency with which we were paid.

My salary for that first year as a surgical intern was $28,500. That was before the days of restricted hours and we easily worked an average of 100 to 120 hours per week throughout a five-year period. The most hours I worked consecutively were eighty-four and the most in one week was 143. Given all the hours, that worked out to be less than five dollars an hour. Minimum wage at the time was $4.25. It was still the most I'd ever earned in my life up to that point. Regardless of the money, I loved it. I really did. I was doing it! I was a no-shit real doctor and had the paper hanging on my wall to prove it.

Back then, there was so much gun violence in North Philadelphia that walking around, I felt like I had a target on my back. Even walking to my car at night didn't feel safe — because it wasn't. People were shot there every day, and rarely did they deserve it.

One particularly ill-fated Friday at noon, as a senior medical student, I was doing a rotation in the surgical ICU when the page operator announced, "Code main lobby, code main lobby." It was lunchtime and we were close, so a classmate and I said we would run down to check it out before we went to grab something to eat. I figured, since it was in the main lobby, a visiting family member had probably passed out and I'd just have to prop their feet up, bring them back, and look like a hero.

We trotted down the stairs, opened the door, and were met with a scene of absolute chaos. People were running, women were crying, and I had no idea what was going on. It was all a blur as I ran full speed into the lobby trying to find the cause of the commotion.

The victim was a twenty-year-old man. I later learned he was a student from the main campus several blocks away. He was there waiting to meet his mother, who was a nurse in the pediatric ICU, for lunch. Apparently, as he was reading a newspaper, a stranger approached him and started asking questions. Maybe they were asking for money or just being weird, but either way, as the student was trying to avoid this conversation the gentleman pulled a pistol out of a brown paper bag and unloaded it five times into the student's head and once into his neck.

As two of the first few medical personnel to arrive at the scene, my classmate Will and I began by throwing chairs to the side, laying him on the floor, and stripping off his clothes. As others arrived we went through our ABCs—Airway, Breathing and Circulation—as fast as we could. We were unsuccessful. He was kept alive long enough to become an organ donor. We never got lunch that day.

Between 1988 and 1997 I attended Temple medical school and residency at the hospital. This was the height of the crack wars and I saw many a gunshot wound, or "9s" as they were called, in individuals who told us they were just walking down the street minding their own business. Their business was often selling crack cocaine, but I was just a lily-white boy from Erie so at first, they could tell me anything and I would believe it. I quickly learned otherwise.

I also saw some of these dealers' clients, including pregnant mothers who were about to give birth to some very unfortunate children. Heroin was popular back then. I treated one homeless gentleman who, after he ran out of veins, went on to skin-pop, or shoot the heroin subcutaneously. I still remember his name, and he wasn't a bad guy. He developed multiple non-healing ulcers that covered the expanse of his legs and arms. The flies in the hot Philadelphia summer couldn't help but lay their eggs in this moist, high-protein environment. We frequently saw this patient in the emergency room when those wounds got infected or the maggots just became too annoying for him to tolerate. It was an eye opener for me, to say the least.

Completing a one-year surgical internship was my first step in becoming an orthopedic surgeon. I truly couldn't believe it. I'd always had good grades, but clearly someone had made a mistake somewhere during the application process. No, really: in my mind, this should have never happened. Step by step, and slowly but surely, I eventually found myself several rungs up the orthopedic surgery ladder of success. I didn't really know I wanted to be an orthopedic surgeon in the beginning. It just sort of happened.

My family was proud of me and so was I. No one stopped me and I was too naïve to really know where I was going. I seemed to be the only one who realized how much this really wasn't meant to be.

While playing doctor in those early days, I wouldn't have been surprised if someone came up to me and said, "You know what? We're sorry, but this whole medical school and residency thing … well, it was actually a huge mistake on our part. It was a paperwork thing, you know, and really meant for someone else."

If I had heard that, I would have quickly replied, "You're right, I kinda figured this would be coming, sorry. I'll get my things."

The surgeons, in general, seemed to me at the time like the biggest, smartest studs in the hospital. I wasn't that. I kept waiting for someone to come up and kick me out, but no one came. No one questioned me. Patients let me examine and operate on them. I tried not to ruffle any feathers for fear that someone would notice and recognize me as the imposter I felt I was. I agreed with everyone and tried to become even more flawless each step of the way. Any little mistake or sign of weakness I was sure was going to be my downfall. This new level of perfection made me look at my old self and think I was a total slouch before. I needed to be perfectly perfect now. I clearly knew I wasn't, but I still had to let on that I was because that's what was expected at this level.

Much attention is paid nowadays to medical residents' and nurses' concerns about microaggressions. Microaggression is defined as "subtle verbal or nonverbal everyday behaviors that arise from unconscious bias, covert prejudice, or hostility." It is a very real thing. In my residency days, however, there was often nothing micro about the aggression we were exposed to. During those years (and for decades before), nothing was subtle or light about the process of learning medicine. Overt macro-aggression was the norm. For us, the goal was to take the pain and borderline abuse without flinching.

I was young, and it seemed like I could go without sleep almost indefinitely; eating was a luxury, and bowel movements only occurred when absolutely necessary. "There are four rules to being a good trauma surgeon," an attending surgeon told us at our opening lecture on trauma surgery and shock. "Eat when you can eat, sleep when you can sleep, shit when you can shit, and don't fuck with the pancreas." Apparently, everything else was negotiable.

While at Temple, I saw some of the worst inner-city gun violence there was. Frequently, young Black men with gunshot wounds walked through our doors or were brought in by the police and EMS. Many were pushed out of a still moving car by their buddies and dropped into our circular parking lot. Temple had one of the highest rates of saves in the country when it came to resuscitating individuals who were considered to be dead on arrival from a gunshot wound to the chest. At the time, the national rate of survival in this scenario was approximately 1 percent. Temple's rate was 9 percent, and that was incredible.

Our numbers were tied to the fact that there was urban blight, poverty, and a raging crack war going on all around us. We were in essence a Level 1 University trauma hospital as North Philly's front line MASH tent. The trauma bay wasn't far from where the victims were shot, so we had the best chance of restoring life.

While cracking the chest open in seconds, cross clamping the aorta and pumping as much blood and fluid into the patient as fast as possible, we would also manually squeeze the heart from the lower point toward the exit pipes, trying to get some oxygen to the brain. We had to do that first to keep the brain alive while we worked on getting the body filled with some type of blood product or intravenous fluid. We had to tank them up first before we could expect the heart to respond to our feverish efforts. I have literally had people's hearts in my hands, trying to pump them back to life. Other times I also, just as literally, had other people's brains on my shoes, but they never made it.

Most concerning to all of us at the time was that while we stomped along in the innumerable puddles of blood throughout the emergency room, there was also an AIDS epidemic flowing in the streets. Despite all this violence and gunshots, the thing we were most worried about was catching HIV from any one of the endlessly bleeding patients. Being shot was, surprisingly, much lower down my list of concerns on a day-to-day basis. Both were definite possibilities.

Since Temple saw so many of these cases, this became routine for us. This was all a part of my superhuman development, but I wasn't even close to being there yet. The head trauma surgeons who directed this process stood back, observing the patient and calmly barking out orders. They were the real superhumans, who knew not to fuck with the pancreas. I was just a brainless cog in that highly efficient timepiece.

After that first year of training, I continued in the orthopedic department, where, whether under the guidance of my attending physicians or not, I did it all. I assisted or performed intramedullary roddings on the shattered femurs of drug dealers. I put fusion rods into the vertebrae of scoliotic children with severe cerebral palsy or spinal cord injuries. I repaired rotator cuff tears and reconstructed anterior cruciate ligaments (ACLs) for Temple's football players. I applied so many casts that my scrubs were often fully splattered with plaster of paris. Standing in an elevator one evening, a visiting patient's family member asked me if that was paint on my scrubs.

I was also privileged to work at the Shriners Hospital for Children during this period as one of their orthopedic surgery residents. By 1996, they had dropped the word "crippled" from their name. Now my Aunt B was no longer crippled, but handicapped, or disabled. She never hesitated to let my father and uncle know that.

"See? You can't call me 'crip' anymore," she'd say. "I'm disabled now." Maybe being called "crip" bothered her more than I realized when I was younger. Either way, her chest was heaving with pride over the fact that I was working there. She would brag to anyone who would listen: "My nephew is working at the Shriners in Philadelphia now."

I had the opportunity to treat many of these inspiring children who were going through surgery and rehabilitation for a wide variety of conditions now that polio was no longer a problem. I witnessed firsthand some of what Aunt B went through and understood more fully why she was so tough. She had been through hell and back at the age of ten.

The orthopedic department had a motto we were expected to live by: "Never complain, never explain, never blame." Everything sat on our own shoulders. We couldn't point fingers at the nurses or offer excuses instead of solutions. Most importantly, we weren't there to whine. The only thing that was accomplished by complaining was being labeled a complainer. Besides, if you did your job—and there was so much to do—you didn't have time to complain. We knew what we had signed up for: long hours, little sleep, high demands, verbal abuse. So why complain?

On a daily basis, my co-residents and I had our minds' and bodies' intensity turned up to eleven on a scale of one to ten. In any given twenty-four-hour period, we would wake up early, familiarize ourselves with the patients' charts and X-rays, and make rounds before heading to conference. There we would present the information to our senior residents and attending physicians, as well as lecture on a specific topic or procedure. We would then run down to the pre-op area to do the days' H&Ps (histories and physicals — part of the initial paperwork completed when you are admitted to the hospital) before the day's surgeries.

If we were efficient enough and finished in time, we might be able to run through the cafeteria to grab a yogurt before surgery. If you weren't efficient, no yogurt for you! If the line was too long or the cashier wasn't right there, we'd stuff the yogurt in a pocket of our lab coats and walk back out the entrance without paying. We didn't have time to wait for a cashier, we had surgery to do! We'd then head up to the OR to scrub and assist in the cases. This went on all day, checking labs and putting in orders between cases, getting the next case ready, and repeating until the scheduled cases were finished.

Once every four days we were also on call. This included answering phone calls, running to the ER to realign the inevitable fractured ankle or wrist, writing a note, heading back up to the OR, and hoping we weren't late for the next case. Days off were rare.

During call nights we stayed in the on-call room in the hospital, sometimes sleeping, sometimes not — and if we did, never for long. When we weren't working on patients, we were preparing for the next morning's presentation or reading up on the cases if we could stay awake. We'd have to collect all the X-rays from that night's work and get ready to present them at conference.

We still tried to sneak in parts of normal life from time to time but normal life was rare. That meant improvising with relationships that might be less than ideal. There were times when a girlfriend would stop by to "have dinner" with us in the on-call room. Most of the time, despite the limited social life and exhausting hours, I loved my life. I loved every moment, every day, without exception. Of course, I was also miserable — I was tired, I was stressed, I neglected everything else — but damn it, I felt like king of the world. No one on the planet was luckier than me to be doing this job.

The amount of time spent, the number of patients we saw, and the daily repetition of the work helped us develop an intuition — a spidey sense, so to speak. In the heat of the moment, it is impossible to always consult your reference material, and there was no internet. Perfect twenty-twenty hindsight — what we call the retrospect-o-scope — isn't ever available to you at the moment of an emergency. Much of what you do is based on protocol so you don't have to think. The protocol is designed to keep you from thinking so you don't miss anything. The problem is that, when faced with an actual patient without a diagnosis and often no history, you *can't* always know which protocol to use. That's when the depth and breadth of your experience comes in. You actually begin to feel it.

What should I do for this patient? Well, it depends. It depends on my spidey senses, given the thousands of bits of information I'm gathering in real time, which tell me something isn't quite right with this patient and I should check something else.

You can't always explain it. There is no textbook for this; you only gain that knowledge through experience.

You also have to become a kind of social chameleon at times, which was something I already had plenty of experience with. My patients didn't always talk to me in the way it's written in books so I had to learn to speak their language. They used words and had mannerisms that were foreign to someone not from their neighborhood. In Philly at that time, everything was a "joint," often pronounced "join." As in, "It's a Spike Lee join." It's a thing that they don't have a specific word for. I heard it used many times in many ways, referring to pretty much everything.

"Doc, you gonna put one a dem cast joins on my boy?"

Translation: "Doctor, are you going to place my son in a cast?"

Another patient asked one of my nurses, "Now for my carpal tunnel surgery, do I need to be euthanized?"

After practically biting her own tongue off, the nurse cleverly replied, "Well, you'll be drowsy but not completely out."

It's a real thing. This cultural clash or divide is everywhere, but very important to know how to cross. Without being able to blend in with the environment in a nonjudgmental manner, you will never get your patients to be honest with you. Whether it was because I grew up with classmates of mixed ethnicities and was from a blue collar family, or because I was adopted, I seemed to be able to assimilate with my patients in Philly much better than many of my more privileged suburban counterparts. Many patients would come to the clinic and tell the secretaries at the front desk something like, "I don't know who saw me. Some white guy." Many of my patients would walk in and say, "Rocco, he's my doctor." I liked that.

I also learned about human error and my own judgment biases. Everyone commits errors and has biases. The key is to know yourself, make up for your shortcomings by compensating in other ways, and try not to repeat your mistakes again. This is especially true if you're tired or the person you're treating is someone you wouldn't normally like. It's not an option to not like someone, even if they are a drug dealer. The patient may be crazy, but crazy people can have bad things happen to them as well. It's important to remain vigilant and not become cavalier.

Missing a diagnosis will potentially harm the patient and burn you the hardest. In order to avoid errors, you have to do a risk analysis of what the worst thing could be, and sometimes rule that out first. You have to dig for what you don't necessarily want to find. In a way it's important to remember you are not treating a person but a *case*. Being "nice" to that person by *not* doing something you know you should and missing the diagnosis is not doing them a favor. Of course, they *are* a person, so it's a fine balance of obligation and compassion.

It seems as though every time I commit a human error or have an undesired outcome, I think about it a lot and put that rock in my sack to carry around with me. All physicians do this. Over the years, that sack gets heavier and heavier as you gain experience in this infinite world of possibilities and exceptions. Your Rolodex of diagnoses gets bigger and bigger as you start to hear similar things explained in similar ways over the years. When you receive a cue you've received in the past, it triggers a memory or a feeling of something that, like divine intervention, pulls you toward the correct diagnosis. You can't know the proper treatment if you don't have the proper diagnosis.

Each year was a progression from the last as we gained more responsibility and freedom to exercise our skills, but the workload didn't really slow down. The days still included presentations, rounding, H&Ps, OR time, clinics, nights in the hospital, and long hours. Compared to the restricted hours of the current residents, it sounds like abuse—and it probably was, but we never looked at it that way. The current residents are still abused as well, or maybe it's more disguised as system mandates and data collection, but there, at least, appears to be an attempt to be aware or minimize it. For us, it was an opportunity to grow. I was motivated significantly by making my family proud but also by seeing how hard, fast, and efficiently my wings could flap.

I called my parents and grandparents every week, if not more, sharing the stories soon after they happened. They both would send me packages of canned clams, tomato sauce, and linguini so I could try to replicate my grandmother's recipes. Unfortunately, I didn't really have the time or energy to cook when I got home so the cans of clams and linguini just kept piling up in my cabinets. My Italian culture was still very important to me, along with the Catholic idealism that came along with it.

Then something happened. It was a typical day and I was on call. I had been in the OR all day and we were just finishing up around midnight. I was dead tired, my shoes hadn't been off all day, and I'm sure I smelled awful. I figured I would walk through the ER to make sure nothing was there waiting for me. The last thing I wanted was to find more work but I learned it was better to check before going to the call room for a break. If I didn't, per

Murphy's Law, just as I was falling asleep, I'd be called again. This was a standard recon mission to prove to myself that I could finally rest.

As I walked into the emergency room hallway, I could see a good deal of activity going on in the trauma bay to my right. The first thing I could see through the door from my approach was the patient's feet. The left one was pointed ninety degrees to the left and the right one ninety degrees to the right. I lost my breath and my heart sank. They were going to need me.

As I walked farther, exposing more of the patient, I could see blood dripping down both ankles and calves. Clearly both of his tibia were fractured and there was bone sticking out of the skin. Bilateral Grade II open tibia fractures. I wanted to cry; I wanted to run away. I wanted my mommy. "Not tonight," I prayed. "Not now, good God, I'm so freaking beat."

I started calculating the time it was going to take to make this man whole again. By the time the trauma team got him through the CT scanner and cleared for surgery, it would be at least 1 a.m., if not later. My stomach was already raw from all the coffee I'd been drinking. My head and feet were killing me, and I could probably poop if I had the chance. I really did not need this right now, but unfortunately, I had to somehow rally.

Okay, close your eyes and relax your body, I told myself. *You can sleep standing up. You'll have at least an hour to go downstairs into the call room and put your feet up before the OR will be ready. We're going to need the rods, maybe an external fixator, the Pulsavac, maybe check his arteries to make sure they're not lacerated as well.*

Now fully on autopilot, all the necessary details for the case were going through my head as I continued to advance, observing more of the patient's body. *Thank God his femurs aren't fractured too, that's good,* I thought. *You've done this a hundred times before, you'll be fine. You don't have to sleep tonight; this is the deal you signed up for. Feel no pain, you can sleep when you get home tomorrow at 6 p.m. You'll sleep through the night and be fine in two days. No big deal.*

Now I could see his torso and his arms—not fractured, good. I still wanted to cry but I wouldn't. The pain in my body was going away as I focused on what I had to fix. The staff in the trauma bay weren't really moving around that fast, I noticed. *What's the deal? Maybe he doesn't have any internal abdominal injuries, maybe it's just his two legs and we can get to the OR sooner and finish before 4 a.m. I still might be able to get an hour or two of sleep.* Then, as his head entered into my field of view, I could see the ventilator was disconnected. *Wait, what? They didn't tube him? He's not breathing? They're not working on him because they're finished? He's dead?*

YES!

I instinctively clenched my fist and visibly shook it in victory. *Nothing for me to do here,* I thought. *I'm going to bed! I'm going to sleep!*

Then it hit me. *I hope no one saw that,* I realized with dread. *Did I really just celebrate the death of another human being just so I could get some sleep? Oh shit, it's happened. I have become dehumanized. Fuck it, I have to sleep. Let me get out of here before someone sees me and wants to ask me another orthopedic question.*

I walked away as quickly as I could. I'm sure I slept like a baby that night and didn't think about the incident for a good while. I was beyond my capabilities. I had often been out of my comfort zone and still managed to function, but I was really tired that night. I had just experienced an emotion that I couldn't really brag about. Was I now officially less human or had I somehow just become superhuman?

I later thought of this moment as I tried to soften it for my soul. Given all that I had seen during those five years of training, was that normal? All the death and injury, all the sleepless nights and coffee, all the putting friends, family, and myself last? Wasn't it about time I thought about what I needed? Finally, I had reached my limit and saw a ceiling to the amount of abuse I could endure.

Of course, I could have cranked it up and gotten it done, but I had definitely realized there was a limit. Armed with my knowledge of the atrocities that men and women have committed throughout history, my response really wasn't that bad. My fist clench and celebration was nothing compared to other possibilities, but I still felt bad. It wasn't like I killed the guy. There really wasn't anything else I could do. Given the situation, the efficient thing was to go to sleep so that I could function better tomorrow for someone else.

Clearly, I wasn't actually celebrating this man's death, but it did look like that and my heart had felt a little lighter. Oh well, I did what I did and hopefully God would understand. Aunt Jill would have said "Weee!" and it should probably have earned me the wooden spoon that night. It would be hard to deny this when reviewing the videotape with St. Peter at the pearly gates. He would say, "There, right there! Isn't that you pumping your fist in a clear sign of celebration over this man's demise?"

"Well, you see, Your Highness, I- I- I was tired," I'd stammer. "I had been up all day. I had been doing that for almost four years straight at the time." It would be hopeless. The tape would tell the truth, and it definitely didn't look good for me.

Sometimes being super doesn't necessarily look so super from the outside. "Super" is also defined by Webster as "... exhibiting the characteristics of its type to an extreme or excessive degree, *super secrecy.*" I thought, did that really make me dehumanized in the sense that it was insensitive and unempathetic? Or, in actuality, did it make me hyper humanized in that those years in residency were so extreme that most other humans would react in a similar way given a similar situation? It had definitely hardened me, but wasn't that also necessary in order to do what I had to do in a disciplined, effective way *for* the patient without allowing my personal emotions to get in my way?

Was I cursed or blessed to be in that position? Had I just been lucky enough to truly see the level to which humans, including myself, can be lowered or raised? Was I traumatized and blinded to my patient's feelings and the satisfaction ratings by which I would later be judged, or was I doing the right thing for the right reasons?

After this episode, how could I piously judge anyone else for his or her actions? I don't truly know another person's experience, their struggles, and all their concurrent ailments contributing to their acts. I'd like to think that all knowledge is power and not just the knowledge that puts us in a good light. Sometimes we cross imaginary borders before we even know it. I do realize that, but for the grace of God or dumb luck, whichever you subscribe to, we could all be seen in the same bad light given the same bad experiences.

We always judge and sometimes we need to do so firmly. We need rules, but given the range of individual perspectives on any given scenario, judging a peer requires a detailed look at the situation. Just as importantly, when there is a shadow of a doubt, shouldn't good humans also give themselves and others an honest appraisal and truly forgive? You can't walk in everyone's shoes, but the more people you're exposed to intimately, the more shoes you can understand. Philly exposed me to a lot more shoes and situations than I ever knew existed growing up in Erie, Pennsylvania, especially as the honored doctor entrusted with people's deepest, darkest secrets.

CHAPTER 4
BLINDSIDED

DESPITE OUR SEEMINGLY DIFFERENT UPBRINGINGS, MY THREE colleagues in residency —John, Ed, and David—and I were also very close. Despite the intense competition and stress, we remained loyal and didn't fight. We hung out a lot both in and out of the hospital. And we had our own code for solving problems.

If two of us were dueling over who had to do some grunt work, we would invoke a game of Rock, Paper, Scissors. For instance, "Who's going to go the ER to admit that femur fracture?" "One, two, three, shoot," always solved the problem.

If there were two or more of us up for a job, it was a little more complicated, but not really. If there was mention of something where it was clear that one of the junior orthopedic residents would be involved, you had to be paying attention. You had to recognize the situation and, as quickly as possible, put your index finger to the side of your nose. It was up to the rest of us to then realize it was game on and get our finger to the nose. The last person to touch his nose was "it."

Those two games afforded us the perfect blend of friendly competition and peaceful harmony. I'd go so far as to say that Rock, Paper, Scissors and finger-to-the-nose rules should be implemented in the United Nations. The world would be a better place.

This level of cooperation was not common in our male-dominated, competitive, orthopedic cage match, where testosterone, machismo, and a cutthroat mentality ran high. Maybe it was because it was an us-versus-them situation: we did fight with our senior residents, however. Not because we were paranoid, but because they *were* trying to kill us.

I can think of at least three instances that involved actual physical fights, with one junior resident rolling on the floor with one senior resident. I didn't get involved in any of that. I didn't yet have the confidence to challenge authority and I just needed to get through residency and stay under the radar.

In addition to wanting us dead, our attending physicians and senior residents were there to teach us. About our medical subspecialty, of course, but also the cultural and behavioral rules of the orthopedic road: "The day isn't over till the work is done," and "Never leave a room until you're sure Latch would be pleased with what you did." John Lachman, MD, or Latch, was our former chairman and orthopedic deity. He was an orthopedic god and father of the Lachman exam, which every orthopedic surgeon uses to determine if the anterior cruciate ligament, or ACL, is ruptured. He was like our Papa. I understood and respected those dynamics.

Our trainers were all truly concerned that we had a lot to learn and it was a *big* responsibility teaching a group of "MO-RONS" like us what orthopedics was supposed to be like. It was absolutely boot camp. We had to be broken down before we could be built back up. What we were doing was serious and we needed to take it seriously. I wouldn't have had it any other way. Being tough on us was how they showed they truly loved us. They didn't care if we liked them or not. They wanted us to respect them and, even more, they wanted us to respect the profession. We ended up doing both.

As tough as it was, residency was a transformative experience. In North Philadelphia, I was far from my comfort zone both professionally and culturally, but it wasn't all work. I had a great time in Philly and many friends and family visited me there. I lost count of how many times I ran up the Rocky Stairs at the Philadelphia Art Museum. And I walked up those stairs more times than I've run up them because, as Rocky notes at the end of *Rocky V*, there "is valuable pictures in this building." It contains some of the best art I've seen.

———

One evening, I had a date that wasn't actually going to take place in the call room. It was a blind date and I was going to take this young lady to a very nice restaurant in Chestnut Hill. I was nervous. First, I could barely afford to take a woman to a nice restaurant. And second, it was rare to meet someone who wasn't in the medical profession.

The streets around the restaurant were filled with couples and families and groups of young college men and women browsing the small specialty shops selling artwork, antiques, and various trendy, artsy clothing.

We met at the designated time and place and awkwardly introduced ourselves. We eventually walked to the restaurant, where I put my name in with the hostess as we got on with the ritual of making conversation with someone we've just met for the first time.

The dinner was moving along and I asked her something about her parents. She stammered a little and said, "Well, it's complicated, because I was adopted."

"Really? That's interesting because so was I!" I replied.

"Really?" she returned.

Suddenly this date became very interesting. Up to that point, I hadn't met anyone else who was adopted. I was excited that we had something substantial to talk about and immediately thought I'd be cute and ask her the question that everyone always asked me.

"Did you ever want to find your real parents?" I asked.

I had always replied with a confident and well-rehearsed, "No, I really never did because my family is just so great." I naïvely expected her to give me the same reply but instead she responded with an equally well rehearsed:

"Well, actually, I did meet my mother."

Her words felt like a slap across my face. *You mean adopted kids really do have real parents that they can find?* I was in shock. *What about the courts and stuff?* My brain scrambled for a way into this now unfamiliar conversation. I think she felt she had to go on because I had nothing intelligent to say.

"Yeah," she continued. "It was interesting because it turns out that the story the nuns told my parents was completely different from the true story."

Really? You had nuns too? I'm not sure if I said that or just thought it because I don't remember verbalizing anything after my initial question about finding her parents.

"It turned out my mother was an alcoholic and lived on the streets and had a really rough life," she said.

I feared what was coming next. Whether I was making any sounds at that point, I'm not sure, but she continued.

"Yeah, the nuns told my adopted parents that my birth parents were two young college kids who couldn't afford to keep a child so they gave me away to a 'good family' who could take better care of me," she went on. "Turns out they used to tell everyone the same story."

I went numb. Eventually, I must have gathered myself and resumed a more natural rhythm and pace to our conversation.

I remember telling her, hesitatingly, "Yeah, that was my story too."

"See! It wasn't true." Once again, it felt like a backhanded boomeranging across my face.

This was the first time in my life I had had a hint that the story I had been told and, in turn, told a thousands of times might not have been true. I was thirty years old, an intelligent medical school graduate and orthopedic resident, and had never thought for one second that the nuns might have lied about my story. That was my sister Lisa's story as well! Now I was punched in the gut with the realization that we had been duped by them. *I should have seen this coming,* I thought. But I hadn't. I had been parroting a lie this whole time, I just didn't know it.

The rest of the dinner was consumed with this discussion. At some point, she told me I needed to get the book called *Journey of the Adopted Self* by Betty Jean Lifton. I didn't even know people wrote books about adoption. I guess I thought that, like getting information about your birth parents, that was illegal too. I'm embarrassed to say that I just believed what I was told and never thought to look it up.

She started to explain some of the book to me and said we should walk down to the Barnes and Noble a few blocks away and pick up a copy. After dinner we did exactly that. I'm not sure how we said goodbye, if we kissed, or if I even said I would call her. I couldn't wait to get home to read this book.

It was this revelation that made this date so extraordinary for me. In fact, it overshadowed everything else: I have complete amnesia about the rest of the date. As a result, I couldn't tell you the first thing about my date: what she did, who she was, or even if I liked her looks or personality.

For adoptees, it turns out this book should come with an advisory label: "Warning! Objects in this book are closer than they appear." I spent the whole next day, a Saturday, walking around Philadelphia, ducking into coffee shops, strolling around parks, and even sitting next to railroad tracks, reading that book. I'd never read a book like that in my life. I was scribbling notes in the margin and underlining sentences as if the book was written just for me. I was blown away. Never had anything made more sense to me in my life.

Lifton talked repeatedly about the closed adoption system. I didn't even know if that was what I had (turns out, it was). Chapter after chapter went on about how this closed system keeps children from knowing their real parents and how it can really mess them up sometimes (my words, not hers). Removing from adopted children the possibility of learning about their origins leaves them with a hole in their center and a feeling they don't really exist. The book talks about adoption trauma being cumulative: starting with the initial separation from the mother at birth, deepens when they find out the people they thought were their parents aren't really, and then is compounded when they're prevented from finding out more about their biological parents.

As Lifton detailed the potential problems these adopted kids can have, I couldn't help but realize that I shared many of the issues she mentioned. Including the hyper vigilance that got me into medical school and residency to begin with! I couldn't put the book down. I related to all of it and was amazed to discover that I could actually be messed up from being adopted. One of my notes at the bottom of page sixty-eight reads, *I don't know how someone who acts and looks like me is accepted or how they best interact with others. What should I say, what should I do? It's all trial and error but I don't ever want to make an error.*

A quick flip through my copy of the book finds underlining on key points on topics such as adoptees not having a "self," not feeling normal, or that they are off balance. In the face of research suggesting that infants under eighteen months show strong attachment to their adoptive mothers, Lifton scoffs, suggesting that this instead may prove only that the adopted child has already learned how to be an imposter.

DAMN! I've been a fraud my whole life, and not just in medical school and residency, I thought.

That Saturday night, there was an orthopedic dinner involving the entire department. The twenty residents, most of the attendings, and emeritus members of the staff were all expected to be there. As one of the honored chief residents, I was also expected to show up. I called one of my buddies and said I was sick. I never, I mean never, missed anything because I was sick. When I've had the flu, I've given myself IVs between cases so I could keep operating. To this day, I have only ever missed one half day of work because of illness.

But *that* night, after reading *that* book, for some reason, I was sick.

I had been so naïve. I realized that I was clueless as to where I came from and it made me feel stupid. There was an actual me before there was a me and I had no idea who he was.

Probably one of the most unusual things for me and many adopted children is that we never really have a *birth day*. Sure, I had a *birthday* that I celebrated every year, but my *birth day* was never really a part of my life or my story. My parents didn't know anything about my birth day. They didn't meet me until I was about six weeks old. I realized at that point that the important day in my life — the day I told everyone who would listen about — was my Gotday. That was the day my parents got me. My birthday was the day that was written on my fake birth certificate from the state with my adoptive name on it. We never talked about my birth day, though. No one really knew anything about that day. My Gotday was the big day, and I loved hearing the story of my Gotday.

"Oh, hun," my mother would swoon. "I remember the day we got you and we took you home all wrapped up in a blanket and showed you to the rest of the family." *That* was the day I began. After that day, I was free to do whatever I wanted.

The other thing my family sometimes told me was that they found me under a rock. My family was into humor when it came to discussing uncomfortable topics and that was my funny history. I knew it probably wasn't true and, of all the abandoned baby jokes in the world, it wasn't the worst or funniest. It was somewhere in the middle. Even thought I knew it was a joke, I spent a lot of time picturing what that rock looked like. My childlike view of it has changed in only one way. If I were going to abandon a baby, I would have chosen a bigger, more protective rock to hide a child under. The other problem with that rock I envisioned was that it was in a desert and there are no deserts in Erie. Nonetheless, I still remember it well.

The only other thing my parents told me about my days in the orphanage was that the nuns called me Larry. They thought that was ridiculous. Why in the world the nuns would ever think to call an Italian kid Larry was hilarious to all of us. They must not have known that Italians don't name their kids Larry. Then again, Italians don't usually name their kids Jack either.

My Gotday was great for me because of all the wonderful things it meant and what I got on that day, such as my love for the Yankees and Italian food. This day was also great for my parents. I'm sure the fact that my mother and father couldn't have their own kids was a tragedy for them and the family. Being a part of a large Italian family, they both felt it was important for them to have children. I'm sure that disappointment was a crushing blow. The fact that they could adopt was a blessing and a wonderful way out of their dilemma. Being able to finally bring home a child must have been so uplifting for them. I'm sure they had their apprehensions, but I never got the impression they ever looked back or regretted one element of their experience. Their hardship probably allowed them to appreciate the process and the opportunity more than most parents who had their own children naturally. My parents loved being parents.

Knowing my parents, I'm know they went to the church they respected and found a solution to their problem. They went along with the authorities and always tried to do the right thing to comply with the rules and regulations of the time. It was, after all, even more of a blessing that my birth parents were coincidentally the same ethnic background as my family. *What are the odds?* I thought. I started to wonder what other facts I didn't know — and what other stories I believed that might not be true.

I was told that the nuns asked my parents for baby photos of themselves before the process started. Apparently, they had a collection of babies and used the photos to match the families with children who looked similar to them. I envisioned a room where my parents sat and the nuns brought me in and said, "This is the one!" From the first time my mother and father saw me, they fell in love, and let's face it, how could they not? The rest was history; I couldn't have been luckier and that's all I needed to know about that.

But now, after the conversation on the blind date and everything I was reading in this book, I didn't know what to believe. Apparently, those nuns had an elaborate network of people they worked with. And who knows what other lies they had told my parents.

Either way, I was told that it was an arduous process. My parents mentioned more than a few times how, for a year during the initial trial period until everything was formalized, the nuns would just show up unannounced to check on them. My father told me, "You were a real pain in the ass to get, you know. I couldn't have a beer for a whole year."

My mother told me I nearly screwed it all up once while they were visiting because I had gotten into a plant she had in the house and made a terrible mess with the soil all over the floor. Thank God, the nuns forgave that.

Reading *The Journey of the Adopted Self* made me realize that the story I so eagerly shared with everyone really wasn't *my* story as much as it was the story of my Gotday. "They got me and then..." The steel door, behind which the rest of me existed, was still locked shut. The story I had told so many times to so many people, regardless of how simplistic it was, now had a big asterisk and blank lines next to it that I couldn't fill in.

It didn't seem to matter. I had gotten this far in life without this information, so was it really necessary? I wasn't sure. It would be great to know, but that would certainly crush my parents' story as well. Their child wouldn't fully be their child anymore, and destroying that story would just be inconsiderate of me. I couldn't do that to them and really didn't know how to go about doing it anyway.

While the orthopedic dinner was going on, I sat in my apartment the rest of that night and into Sunday paralyzed, reading, and thinking. I had never experienced anything like this in my life. I couldn't go back to the rat race on Monday morning still in this stupor. By Sunday evening, I had rationalized that this book was just like a horoscope. You could read any sign and find a way to apply it to you whether your birthdate matched it or not. I decided the author had something political to prove against the closed adoption system. After all, I never seemed to have any problems until I read the book. It was bringing up issues with drug and alcohol abuse, and I never did drugs or abused alcohol. Sure, I drank like everyone else I grew up with, but no one would accuse me of being an alcoholic. *Maybe that was a part of my fraud?* I thought. I didn't know what to think or how much I was even fooling myself. It just seemed like the book brought up all these problems that I didn't have. If anyone read it, they would wonder if they had these problems too. Everyone has some of these insecurities. Adoption was never really a problem for me.

I had to bury this shit and quick. I put the book down and never went out with that girl again. It was too painful, and I had to work the next day.

My story changed a little after that. From then on, I would tell the same story with an asterisk. "Well, the nuns told my parents this but it turns out that it's probably not true," I planned to say. "I still have a really great family and story and well, you know, nuns can sometimes lie to make things sound rosy."

I had to carry it all in the back of my head but outwardly it didn't really change anything. I went back trying to be Jack and Dr. Rocco, whoever they were.

But I couldn't stop thinking about it and the curiosity slowly crept back. The following week, I was exploring the still-infantile America Online (AOL). It was 1997 and I came across an adoption registry. I put out my first feeler for locating my birth mother. I listed my name, birthdate, place of birth, and contact information.

About two weeks later, I received a message in the office on a yellow sticky note: "Dr. R, please call Amy at 215-555-5555. She says she's an old friend."

My wheels were turning. An old friend? Now, that was interesting. But the area code was 215, which is Philadelphia. Erie, where most of my old friends were, was 814. I knew an Amy from Pittsburgh, which was 412, but I didn't have any old friends by that name in 215.

Oh my God, I thought. *This internet shit actually works!* I knew immediately that Amy was my birth mother's name and she was replying to my registry inquiry. She must have been following me, like a guardian angel, this whole time and knew everything there was to know about me. She knew exactly where to find me and was just waiting for me to look before she revealed herself. I was so excited. And scared to death. I couldn't believe that she was here, in area code 215, and I had never tried to look. Maybe she moved around with me, like a stalker, watching me from time to time as I went about my life. My mind was racing.

I went home and slowly talked myself into dialing the number. I got an answering machine and listened to her voice. As I listened, there was no doubt: she sounded just like me. I hung up. I called back a little later and listened to the voice again. She really did sound nice, and smart and funny, and not like an alcoholic at all. I could tell by her voice that she was pretty and had long black Italian hair. I could picture her and was amazed that she looked exactly like a female version of me. I hung up.

I'm not sure how many times I called back and hung up but eventually an actual person picked up.

"Hello," the now-familiar voice said.

"Hi," I said. "This is Jack. You called me?"

"Who?" she replied.

"Jack, Jack Rocco. You left a message for 'Dr. R' at Temple's orthopedic office for me?"

"Oh, yeah!" she replied. "That was me, but that was for Dr. Resnik. They must have given it to the wrong Dr. R."

"Oh, that's funny! Okay, I'm sorry for that. I'll give him your number," I replied with a cheerfulness I didn't feel.

I was both relieved and disappointed. I didn't have time for all this up and down emotional nonsense. I had doctoring to do. After all this, I decided that finding my mother was just an unnecessary distraction.

CHAPTER 5
SOLDIERING ON

DURING RESIDENCY, BASIC LIVING EXPENSES TOOK UP A GOOD DEAL OF my salary, and after a brief period, my school loan payments would kick in or I'd be forced into forbearance. In order to make a little more cash, I looked into selling my body. Unfortunately, the only interested party was the United States Air Force.

Once again, I didn't know exactly what I was getting myself into. A recruiter showed up at the hospital one day to buy the residents lunch and tell us about opportunities to practice within the military. I had always wanted to travel, and I felt I needed more time to develop my skills before being thrown into the high-pressure situation of running a private practice. I think the idea of a physician's salary made me a little nervous as well—I had never known anyone growing up who made that kind of money and was quite apprehensive about taking that leap. The Air Force sounded like a good way to delay thinking about that and soften the transition. After a few weeks, I signed up for the monthly stipends and annual bonus and my immediate financial needs were met.

I was commissioned a captain before I even set foot on a military base. I received credit for college, medical school, and residency as years in service. As a result of all the years of school and training, after only one year of active duty, I would then be eligible for the rank of major. If you go the typical route, it takes at least ten years in the military to get that rank. Most captains and majors know what they're doing; I knew very little about the military. My "years in service" were accrued during civilian endeavors. Benjamin Franklin "Hawkeye" Pierce would probably best describe me as a military doctor. At the time, he was the only captain/military doctor I could identify. I'm sure Alan Alda's character on *MASH* influenced me much more than he should have, given that he was fictitious and I was real. Well, sort of.

Over the next few years of residency, I had plenty of time to consider where I wanted to spend my active duty. I eventually decided to try to experience something unique outside the country. There were only a few bases available overseas for orthopedics. European bases were much more desirable and difficult to come by. I selected Misawa Air Base Japan as my first choice for preferred duty station. And got it.

Misawa wasn't a highly sought-after assignment. Located at the northern tip of the main island of Honshu, Japan, it was an important location as an F-16 hub and an intelligence base. Unlike the bustling Tokyo, Misawa is fairly rural and far enough north that the winters can be brutal. I wasn't bothered by the cold. We were also surrounded by a number of fairly active political arenas, including Russia to the northwest, North Korea directly west, and China further inland.

It was a solo position, so I would be working by myself, the only orthopedic surgeon on a base of around twelve thousand military personnel and their families. I'm sure that combination of factors frightened a great number of the younger physicians, and the more experienced surgeons usually preferred a larger overseas or stateside base to build their career. I had a great foundation from Temple and believed I was ready for Misawa. I definitely had a good deal of growing to do and Japan would allow me to make the quantum leap I needed to truly earn my wings. The common theme of making things difficult for myself played into this decision too. Most importantly, I chose this move because I was young, naïve, and clueless as to what the hell I was doing. This is not always a bad thing.

When I told my mother I was moving to Japan, she was crushed. "Aww, hun. Japan? Really?"

"Ma, it'll be a great experience!" I assured her.

"Haven't you had enough experiences already?" was her reply.

My father dug deep into his cache of emotions and came out with something to the effect of "Jesus Christ, Jack. Japan? I'm never gonna see you now. How are you gonna eat that food?"

Maybe they were right, but it was too late. I was committed. During an introductory two-week field training exercise, I sent a photo of myself all geared up in my government-issued equipment back to the family. I had on my camouflaged chemical suit, flak vest, and gas mask hanging down from my utility belt. The Kevlar helmet was positioned so neatly on my head I looked like a hardass.

My mother later told me that when she showed Papa the picture, he said: "Look at him. He's still having fun." And I was. By the time Papa was thirty-one, he was deep into his grown-up life with a family and children. At the same age, I was single and traveling the world playing soldier. He loved it.

During officer training at Maxwell Air Force Base in Montgomery, Alabama, I was introduced to the unofficial AF motto "Semper Gumby." Our trainer explained to us that in military war situations—and air battles in particular—you weren't always going to know what to expect but had to be flexible in your approach in order to survive. The cartoon character Gumby best characterized that flexibility, and I liked that. We often flew by the seat of our pants at Temple. On any given day, it was impossible to know what to expect, so we had to be nimble and flexible. Despite the claim of Semper Gumby, however, things were much more structured in the Air Force.

As a young resident at Temple, I came up behind and looked up to many more senior attending physicians. In the Air Force, I was considered one of the older guys. I was a captain and chairman of the orthopedic surgery department. Turns out, there really wasn't a chairman position. In a strange twist, the physician assistant (PA) assigned to support me, Stephen Kette, actually had the title of chief because he outranked me by a few months. He made up the title of chairman for me to keep the peace. In civilian life, doctors outrank PAs, but in the military, Kette was the one writing my progress reports as my supervisor. It was a little backwards. But with his military experience, he was better suited to the administrative requirements of that position. He was a competent, skilled, and caring individual who kept me out of a lot of trouble.

My first few months were a blur. It wasn't uncommon for me to walk into the hospital, confident in my brand-new uniform and rank, only to have some young airman come up to me and say, "Captain, your name tag is on the wrong side of your shirt." I would stumble to put it on the other side before someone of higher rank noticed.

I wasn't used to having to obey all these rules and procedures. Even though I knew there was a right way to do things, I didn't think it mattered what you looked like doing them. I was green and destined to fail in my attempts to figure out why the rules were the way they were, but I was not alone. No one really knew why he or she was doing anything a certain way, but they were going to do it that way come hell or high water. Their career depended on it.

Ironically, I could have benefited from wearing my flak vest more in Philly than I did in the military. I didn't witness any gunshots in the military; it was a time of peace. Most of what we did in Misawa was for training—and that was good. We did suffer a few F-16 crashes during training missions, which can be worse than a gunshot wound. I didn't join the Air Force to see battle. I was just poor and needed the money. I didn't intend to work my way up through the ranks, so I settled into my little office in the basement of the hospital and focused on the same thing we were all focused on: "doing more with less" in our underfunded branch.

I looked forward to coming up with inventive ways for doing a good job with minimal resources.

In my heart, my main alliance was to the profession of medicine—not the military. My office was far away from Tiptoe Alley — the row of offices where all the higher-ranking hospital leaders were situated. I went there as little as possible. Given my naïveté and rebellious nature, I figured that eventually I was going to be called up there for some reason. Still, I was surprised when my first brush-up with the brass occurred and Tiptoe Alley came to me.

"You are a very young captain, aren't you?" the lieutenant colonel barked at me as he closed the door to my small office behind him. It was meant to be a private conversation, but I have no doubt everyone outside of the flimsy drywalled room heard every word we said. He was at least six inches taller than me, so even though we were both standing, he towered over me as he yelled. I knew exactly what this was all about.

Earlier that morning, the door to my exam room had been thrust open and the sanctity of my doctor/patient relationship violated. I was in the middle of examining a patient's knee when the same lieutenant colonel suddenly and forcefully entered.

"Captain Rocco, what's the situation with this emergency air-evac patient you're trying to send to Hawaii?" he blurted.

"Yeah, he's got an unstable femoral neck and shaft fracture, so I have to send him to Tripler," I explained with my current patient's knee still in my hands.

"And he needs to go today?" he questioned.

"Yes, it's already a week old and I need to get him there ASAP," I told him.

"I don't believe that," he replied dismissively.

I was starting to get a little annoyed with this interruption and the questioning of my medical authority in the middle of my exam. "Well, I do," I reasserted.

"I've known a lot of orthopedic surgeons in my life and I don't think that constitutes an emergency," he replied.

"Well, I'm the one you have here now and I do," I repeated in disbelief, wondering, *What kind of bizarro world am I practicing in here?* He stormed out just as quickly as he'd entered and I turned back to the patient, trying to remember where I was.

I completed my exam but was fuming. He'd burst into my private exam room, questioned my decision-making in front of a patient, and had no idea what he was talking about. I boiled over this for the rest of the morning. By lunchtime, I couldn't take it anymore and thought he needed to hear my thoughts. An email would suffice. The internet and emails were new at that time and I hadn't gotten the memo yet that said, "Never send angry emails— especially to lieutenant colonels." I basically told him three things:

1. Never burst into my exam room while I'm with a patient.

2. Never question me in front of patients or staff.

3. He was just a flight surgeon, and medically, I was there to make the orthopedic decisions because he wasn't qualified to do so.

This was a far cry from my first days as a surgical intern, when I would have easily packed up my bags and left if someone had told me my acceptance was an accident. Somewhere in my five years of intense exposure to one of the toughest neighborhoods in Philadelphia, I had become hardened steel.

I was scared to death being in Misawa by myself, but the orthopedic department was my responsibility and I took it seriously. This tiny ship was not going down under my watch. As the only orthopedist on base, it seemed like I was all alone in trying to maintain the efficiency of this small cog within the Air Force's greater mission. If I backed down, I would lose all credibility for the rest of my time on base. I may have been out of my element in the military, but I was completely within my realm of orthopedics.

I discussed the situation with Kette and Tech Sergeant Holland, the noncommissioned officer in charge (NCOIC). They agreed that he was wrong, but kindly warned me that the email was probably not the best way to bring that up with him. Within an hour, the door to my clinic burst open and there he was, again, yelling at me about being a "very young captain."

"I guess you got my email," I wanted to say, but instead replied, "This has nothing to do with rank, sir."

He moved even closer and opened his mouth even wider a second time to roar: "Yes, but you *are* a very young captain, aren't you?"

"This still has nothing to do with rank," I said intently and calmly held my ground. He was an experienced lieutenant colonel and flight surgeon. I had only been a captain for six months. The United States Air Force had brought me on to exercise my orthopedic skills. He was apparently brought on to exercise his leadership skills. We were both correct.

The patient in question was a twenty-year-old airman who, under the influence of alcohol, crashed his car into a Japanese rice field. (The Japanese didn't like that because the car fuel and oil damaged their rice fields for years to come.) The patient fractured his femoral shaft and his femoral neck, both significant injuries. We didn't have the necessary equipment to fix that combination of injuries. I did my best to improvise, but my solution wasn't holding. He needed to be sent to the nearest advanced trauma hospital, more than four thousand miles away in Hawaii.

I ran it by my NCOIC and he informed me that there was a C-130 air-evac plane coming later that day. If I made it "stat," the patient could get on the plane the same day. If I didn't do it immediately, we would have to wait a week or call another plane specifically for this patient. It made more sense to make the patient "stat" and get him on the plane that was going to be here soon. The lieutenant colonel apparently didn't like that idea and I wasn't sure why.

"I know you're new to the Air Force and don't seem to understand how things work around here," he told me. He was in charge of arranging for transport to Hawaii and I apparently hadn't gone through the proper channels in my decision. Given our difference in rank, he was expecting me to start groveling, but as the patient's advocate, I stood my ground.

"This kid has a femoral neck fracture and if that isn't stabilized, the bone will die and he'll need a hip replacement," I explained. "You don't want a twenty-year-old to get a hip replacement, do you?"

I was pissed because I was doing my best and didn't feel I should have to explain this to him. I could have been nice, but he drew first blood by violating my three points of light. I was on a roll and couldn't stop my mouth.

"I am stuck here in the middle of nowhere with limited equipment and I am doing my best. If I think I need to send a patient out, they need to go out," I explained, just how I think Hawkeye would have.

"Yeah, but that happened a week ago," he replied. "Why didn't you send him out then?"

"Because it was nondisplaced. I thought I could hold it with what we had but it was starting to move," I told him.

"It costs $30,000 to call a plane up here for that. Can't it wait?" he asked.

"There's already a plane coming today. Tech Sergeant Holland said if I made him 'stat' we could get him on that plane today."

"So there is already a plane coming?" he asked.

"Yes, and I didn't want him to wait another week."

"Oh," he retreated. And I pounced.

"So you didn't know that there was a plane already coming? You thought I called it specifically for this patient?"

"Yes," he admitted, embarrassed.

"Well, that's the problem. You jumped the gun and came running down here to bawl me out without knowing the situation," I snapped. I was in full-out offensive kill mode, with my orthopedic leadership wings soaring over the crystal blue horizon.

"All right then," he relented. "That's fine."

I escorted him out of my office and as he walked away, I asked, "So are we still friends?"

"Yes, Jack. We're friends." I didn't believe that for a second.

He clearly didn't like how that conversation went. Our chief medical officer, a full bird colonel, confided in me later that the lieutenant colonel told him, "Watch Rocco. He's a troublemaker." He wasn't wrong, but neither was I.

Having just experienced my first full-on culture clash— between military protocol and medical prowess—I had the feeling this could be the first of many. I was learning the hard way that rules and structure are important but also sometimes arbitrary. These cultural norms need to be followed but sometimes they also need to be challenged. There is a right and a wrong way to challenge them but the right way isn't always practical in the heat of the battle. Sometimes you need to walk on the fringe—not really bad, not really good, but just flexible enough to go from side to side. That's how I was starting to interpret Semper Gumby.

From that moment, to make things less complicated, I decided I needed to stay as far away from military leaders as possible. If I didn't, I might just find myself turning big rocks into little rocks at the United States Disciplinary Barracks in Leavenworth, Kansas.

With the hope of enhancing my military experience, I decided to try to focus more on building a relationship with my Japanese orthopedic colleagues. Being the sole orthopedic surgeon straight out of a civilian residency program on an underfunded base was much more difficult than I imagined. I didn't always have the equipment I needed or the peers to run ideas by. I was far away from any other orthopedist and was expected to be the expert on everything. The next military base was four hundred miles away in Tokyo, and beyond that it was Hawaii. I contacted a number of Japanese orthopedic surgeons in town but wasn't successful in establishing a relationship because of language and cultural barriers. It was frustrating.

My best friend at the time was Lucas "Buzz" Landreneau. He was a sassy, smart, and streetwise captain from New Orleans in the Judge Advocate General office—a JAG. I was single, and most of the other doctors and nurses in the hospital were married. The single F-16 pilots were like a high school football team: They usually kept to themselves. The entire JAG office was comprised of single guys so I ended up hanging with them fairly often.

I learned so much about the military from a legal perspective from the JAGs. War wasn't just a bang-bang, shoot 'em up affair. It was a contractual obligation ordered through Congress and it involved not just a show of force, but also multiple complicated geopolitical structures, laws of engagement, Status of Forces Agreements, and a whole host of other legal issues. For the first time in my life, I was exposed to a behind-the-scenes view of government workings—often over a bottle of Bombay Sapphire Gin. Apparently, that's what lawyers drink. Doctors and lawyers hanging out together was not what I expected from my military experience.

Buzz and I went on a number of boondoggles together during those years. One such trip involved getting on a C-130 to Osan Air Force base in Korea. Osan and Itaewon, in Seoul, were known for being great places to shop. You could get all your Christmas presents, ship them back to yourself or your family at the local military post office, and be done with it. All the women in my family had knock-off Coach purses, Japanese trinkets, and ceramic wares as a result.

While on one of our first trips, we ran into a guy named Lonnie. Lonnie was a thirty-five-year-old Black master sergeant with a great, wide-open personality, and welcoming smile. We met Lonnie while waiting for our plane in the terminal and we all hit it off. Officers and enlisted men weren't allowed to socialize because it violated fraternization rules, and Buzz complied. So did I, for the most part.

After a day of shopping in Osan, we happened to run into Lonnie again at a local drinking establishment. We had a few drinks and got to know each other better. He thought we were less highbrow and formal than the other JAGs and doctors he'd met. I thought he was hilarious, laid back, and well-seasoned in the ways of the military and being overseas. After that trip, I bumped into him a few more times—once while I was coming out of a Japanese language class, and then again at the gym. Eventually we started hanging out.

Lonnie knew of a great city where we could go and experience some of the Japanese nightlife. It wasn't anywhere near our Podunk little base and we wouldn't be around other military members. We both knew hanging out was considered inappropriate and was a small step over the fraternization line. He wasn't in my chain of command, and as far as I was concerned, it was just two guys going out to travel, drink, and maybe find girls.

We eventually got together on a fairly regular basis. Lonnie told me he was dating a Japanese woman whose mother owned a hospital. I didn't believe him and figured she was head nurse or an administrator or something. I later found out the mother was one of the wealthiest individuals in that town, the highest-earning female—and, yes, part owner of a Japanese hospital. That was *very* unusual for Japan, a predominantly male-dominated society. Lonnie had clearly hit the jackpot. His girlfriend's mother did not know, however, that her daughter was dating a Black American enlisted man. That would not have been accepted.

One day Lonnie came up to me at the gym and said he talked to his girlfriend about me and the orthopedic doctors at her hospital wanted to meet me. Bingo, the seal was broken! I started going to their hospital every other week. It was about thirty miles away, in the same town where Buzz lived (we both lived off base to assimilate into the culture even more).

The other doctors spoke English but I tried to use as much of my Japanese as possible. We exchanged case studies and I had the privilege of scrubbing in with them on surgeries. They helped me out several times by letting me have some equipment and supplies I needed for special cases. I was warned by some of my military colleagues not to tell anyone I was operating with and getting equipment from a Japanese hospital because that probably wouldn't be approved. I quickly learned a familiar military concept: "It's better to beg for forgiveness than to ask for permission." I didn't see anything wrong with accepting their help. It was great for my patients and helped me out quite a bit as well. I was doing more with less.

After our meetings, we'd go for dinner and drinks. I was getting an inside view of Japanese culture. Despite my father's fears, I ate more disgusting versions of sushi than most people usually want to hear about. I swallowed live shrimp, raw whale, and horsemeat, virgin cow uterus, and was even tricked into sampling some raw salmon sperm sac. Don't judge! This was a far stretch from the boy who turned his nose up at any pizza with ham and pineapple or feta cheese toppings, sticking instead to the basic cheese and pepperoni.

My Japanese was improving, and I could sit around all night trying to speak Japanese and learning to listen as well. I was invited to golf outings where there would be forty-seven Japanese physicians, lawyers, and businessmen from the area playing together. It was a fantastic experience.

Several months later, I learned of a local educational conference that was occurring across the prefecture at Hirosaki University. I asked if I could go and my colleagues secured my invitation. Jessie Jupiter, MD, from Mass General Hospital in Boston, was going to be the visiting lecturer. I knew of him from his many published articles and textbooks and was excited to meet him in person.

Awkwardly, I walked into the conference by myself as the only other American. I wasn't hard to pick out. I entered an elevator and ran into an older Japanese gentleman. I politely bowed and said "Konichiwa," not knowing if he spoke English. He returned my bow and, in almost perfect British English, said, "I understand you're from the American air base."

"Yes, I am," I confirmed. It turned out he was the sitting president of the International Hand Society at the time. He took me to where I needed to go and introduced me to who I needed to meet, including Dr. Jupiter!

I met Satoshi Toh, MD, who was a fairly young hand surgeon favored to become the next chairman of the orthopedic department. I attended the conference as well as the after-conference refreshment session. As a now-special guest from America, I was then invited to the after-refreshment session, which included much better food and drink, with only a few select attendees. From there we went to the after-party, which included a good deal of Japanese whiskey and karaoke singing by all members of the party, including myself and Dr. Toh. He sang Tony Bennett's "I Left My Heart in San Francisco" especially for me to show off his English singing abilities, which was impressive considering it was 2 a.m.

This was the start of an invaluable professional and cultural immersion program the likes of which could never be duplicated. Over the next few years, I went to a number of national conferences as the token American white boy in Toh's entourage. In life, we might not be who we thought we were, but we can often be who we want to be. At this moment in time, my small-town identity was thrust onto an international stage. All of my years of experience were melding together to represent both myself and my country with every interaction.

I also met Loris Pegoli, MD, a young orthopedic surgeon from Genoa, Italy, who was doing a hand surgery fellowship with Dr. Toh. It was a an honor to be interacting and working with this mixed international group on the other side of the world. Loris and I also became friends. He would come to Misawa on occasion and stay with me to tour the base, observe surgery, and go out to the local clubs after work. He told me, "Jack, I want to date an American soldier." This struck me as humorous because it sounded like he meant a male but he clearly meant a female. Unfortunately, we never found anyone for him.

At one of these national conferences we attended in Kyoto, a group of us went out after the lectures for a few drinks. Loris was drawing a surgical procedure on the back of a cocktail napkin. I looked around. I was having drinks with the whole world. The president of the International Hand Society was there again, so was the president of the Japanese Hand Society, and the president of the American Hand Society. There was a German surgeon teaching a Brazilian surgeon about what he did. A physician from Ecuador was joking with another well-known surgeon from Australia. It was incredible.

They were all the best in the world and they were interacting with such beautiful ease. They all had different languages, mannerisms, and personalities, which epitomized their local culture. They were all doing it in their own style and it was just fine. No arguments, no judgments, no wars, no hard feelings— because we were all the best doctors in our own respective domains, me included. I was the best, and only, American military doctor in the group and was humbled to be there. Being an adopted kid from an American industrial blue-collar town made the experience even headier for me.

Meeting and working so closely with some of the world's orthopedic surgeons in an environment far from home didn't seem unusual or difficult at all. We shared the commonality of our trade, our human compassion for our patients, and the quality of care we provided. We all did things a little differently, but there were more things that were the same. The food, the culture, the dress, and the national ethnic differences fell to the wayside. Each of these physicians had children and loved ones and struggled through the politics of their local environments or government requirements. We could easily sympathize and empathize with one another. We all left the conference as better physicians and people.

Later that week, I had the opportunity to have a conversation with a *geisha*. She was in a piano bar with a Japanese man who trained and did research at Emory University in Atlanta. As I went to get a drink, he struck up a conversation with me in English. Eventually, I humbly recognized his date, and speaking in Japanese, expressed to her my appreciation for her art. After reading the novel *Memoirs of a Geisha,* I felt I had learned a fair amount about *geisha* and their lives. She shared with me that she and her colleagues didn't like the book because it gave Americans the idea that all *geisha* were sold into the trade by their parents. I assured her that this was not the case and that most Americans realized it was only a representation of past times and that it was much different now. It was amazing to me that, despite having grown up in such humble beginnings in Erie, I was now speaking to a *geisha* in Kyoto about American literature. It seemed impossible.

All of this started with me uncomfortably hanging out with a group of JAGs, one boondoggle trip to Korea with Buzz, an *inappropriate* relationship with a Black enlisted man who was having an *inappropriate* relationship with a wealthy Japanese woman's daughter. Despite having tried the traditional paths to appropriate relationships with the local orthopedists, I ended up having further *inappropriate* relationships with a group of Japanese orthopedic surgeons who provided me with *unauthorized* medical supplies to treat my patients.

I eventually helped those physicians by rewriting and editing their research articles so they would be better worded for submission to America's top orthopedic journals. We had five papers published during that period. The first paper I helped rewrite for them was published in *The Journal of Bone and Joint Surgery*, America's top orthopedic journal. It was the first article ever to be published in *JBJS* from Hirosaki University. The lead author on the paper was a surgeon who couldn't have bowed lower when he met me. His nose was practically on the ground. The additional research coming out of his department also sealed the deal for Toh becoming the new chairman. Was all of that inappropriate? It never felt that way.

Was all of this accomplished by a fraud or imposter who didn't know who he was? That's what Betty Jean Lifton, the author of *Journey of the Adopted Self*, would have said. Maybe my chameleon superpowers stemming from being adopted actually helped. Either way, it helped me survive those years in the Air Force. My intentions were good — and they rarely led me astray, even in the most uncomfortable of situations.

The Japanese have a phrase, *ichigo ichie*, which means a once-in-a-lifetime experience. During another weekend, months later, I had the chance to experience my *ichigo ichie*. I was sitting on a packed Shinkansen (bullet train) coming back from Tokyo. Every seat was taken except for the one to my left. No one liked sitting next to the foreigner. At one of our stops, the last guy you would want sitting next to you entered the train and I knew he had his eyes fixed on being my neighbor. He was old and shuffling, dressed in rags, and looked like he hadn't showered in a while.

As he took his seat he said, "Herro."

Oh great, he speaks English too, I thought. "Konichiwa," I replied.

"It's okay, I smoke?" he then asked.

"Hai," I assured him. *This is going to be a long, painful, smelly train ride*, I thought.

"You GI?" he asked.

"Hai," I confirmed, as I tried to avoid this possibly annoying conversation. I was a little tired from the weekend in Tokyo and just wanted to sleep.

"I GI too," he told me. "I was fi-ta pirot."

"Fighter pilot?" I asked, wanting to be sure I could understand his broken English.

"Hai," he confirmed.

"Itsu (when)?" I asked, realizing he was really old and didn't look like any fighter pilot I'd ever met.

"World War," he told me.

"Really?" This guy sitting next to me was a freaking World War II pilot? I was suddenly awake.

He went on with his story. He was nineteen when the bombs fell, and the war ended. He hadn't seen much action but did see some and was grateful that it ended.

"Sank you," he told me.

"Thank me? For what?" I wondered.

"Peace is better," he explained. "Japan was bad, war is bad, we are better now."

To him, I represented everything that he knew of America, its military, and soldiers. It wasn't necessarily me he was thanking but my American history and, as America's representative, I was honored to accept it. He wanted me to be proud and I didn't want to disappoint him. I was proud. Papa was also proud when I told him that story.

I asked him everything I could fit into our brief encounter. I had been to the Hiroshima Peace Memorial Museum several months earlier and cried when I saw the photos, drawings, and artifacts from that day. I cringed when I realized the target was a purely civilian one. It was aimed at people who looked just like the ones I had grown to love by living among them over the past few years. I'd grown to appreciate the Japanese culture and food and people and history. I felt as though I was a little Japanese myself as a result. It horrified me that we dropped such a catastrophic bomb on them and it wasn't even a military target. My JAG brothers would have never approved of that now.

I asked him what he thought about the bomb.

"I think it was necessary because Japan was bad back then but things are better now with you here," he said.

I was floored. I was expecting him to hate me for what my country had done. I was expecting to hear how he lost friends in the war to American bombs or gunfire. I was expecting to hear how his family went through innumerable hardships as a result of the war. Instead, he felt it was necessary to make his country better in the long run? The Japanese are notoriously courteous, but this seemed heartfelt, like he honestly meant it.

We carried on our conversation and I felt a bond developing with this man that I initially didn't want to sit next to me. I realized that, when he saw me, he was excited and interested to sit next to an American and practice his English. He took the opportunity to thank me for something decades earlier that I had nothing to do with and I had almost ignored him. I felt ashamed.

When we arrived at his stop, we stood up and shook hands with both hands clasped around each other, not just one.

"Sank you, sank you, sank you," he kept saying.

He got off the train and shuffled down the platform to the window where I sat. He waved and his eyes followed the train as it started down the track. We were like two lovers who knew we'd never see each other again. It was sad but it was also uplifting. We'd shared a connection, a great conversation, our interaction a representation of two iconic nations healed from events a long time ago. How could I ever have expected to receive something this precious?

Those four years in Japan ended up accounting for some of the best years of my life and were a huge part of who I later became. Something I decided to do largely for the money — to join the military and serve in Japan — taught me more about the world, people, and politics than I ever could have imagined. They exposed me to a different way of thinking—both in the military and regarding Asian cultures. The friends and colleagues I met then have remained a big part of my life. I've since met innumerable military veterans with whom I now share the special bond of shared service. I've also been more open to conversations with people from Japan, Korea, Australia, Russia, and South America — countries and cultures that don't seem scary to me anymore. I have personal friends, acquaintances, and experiences with people from all over the world and they are so much more similar to me than they are different.

That experience of cultural immersion effectively broke down personal barriers and biases about which I had been previously unaware. I learned that you could bring your culture with you, just love it and share it, in a spirit of shared curiosity and appreciation without imposing it on anyone else. What may be boring or routine to me might be engrossing to someone else. I stood to learn a lot from others, provided I don't judge.

Semper Gumby, my friend.

PART TWO
NATURE

"Choose only one master: nature."

REMBRANDT

CHAPTER 6
SHE YAWNS LIKE ME

ON SEPTEMBER 13, 2001, I WAS SCHEDULED TO GO ON A JOYRIDE IN AN F-16 as part of a farewell package before departing from the military. That flight was cancelled because of the attack on the twin towers two days earlier. After four years of military service, my last official day in the Air Force was on September 30 — just one day before Congress issued a stop-loss order that would've required me to stay.

Part of me felt like I was abandoning everyone. I had enjoyed the peace and joy of living overseas under Uncle Sam's arm and now that he and all my friends in the Air Force really needed me, I was leaving. All my possessions (the military calls them "household goods") were already packed up and headed to the states by September 11, so I had no choice.

Earlier in the year, I had signed a contract to join a private practice with one of my co-residents from Temple. David was working just outside of Providence, Rhode Island—in Johnston, to be exact. The Federal Hill section of Providence was their Little Italy. There were a many authentic Italian restaurants and grocery stores filled with the smell of fresh sharp provolone cheese and patrons with that classic Italian swagger I knew so well. These Italians, however, being so close to Boston, were actually Red Sox fans. I didn't realize that was allowed.

Johnston was even more Italian than Providence. Many of my patients and coworkers were Italian. I pretty much fell right into place in that environment—but not completely. Rhode Island has this crazy half-Boston, half-New York accent that I had a hard time understanding, at first. During my first month, one of the nurses came into my office after clinic and said, "Doc, jagetcha chaats?"

"Pardon me?" I asked.

"Ya chaats, jagetcha chaats?" she repeated.

"I'm sorry, I don't understand," I replied again. *JA GET CHA CHAATS*, I repeated in my head, trying to find a word in that sentence. I thought I was having a stroke because it seemed like she was speaking English but I couldn't understand any of it. It was delivered in a crazy-fast burst of sounds I'd never heard come out of a human mouth before. I thought my brain was somehow mixing my English comprehension with the Japanese comprehension and I could no longer understand either.

"Yourrrr charrrts, did you get yourrr charrrts," she slowly corrected herself, making sure to enunciate the Rs this time.

"*Oh!* My charts. Yes, I got them. Thank you," I replied. *For God's sake, I understand the Japanese better than I understand Rhode Islanders*, I thought.

Coming back to the states was surprisingly difficult. Now, when patients or friends learned I was in the military, they thanked me for my service. I was never thanked for my service when I was *in* the military. But now we were at war, and I was thanked. I accepted it for my fellow military buddies but didn't feel I deserved thanks for what they now had to go through. I ruminated on that a lot.

There was also a clash between the narrow way that I viewed the world before I left America and the broader understanding I had of the world after living overseas. The people I initially looked at as different or weird during my life abroad were really mostly the same as those back home in America. Sure, billions of people didn't know anything about the NFL or Britney Spears. Still, they had other preoccupations, like sumo wrestling or K-pop. At the end of the day, no matter where I was, people had the same core concerns: their health, their children, their culture, and their prosperity.

Many of my new coworkers hadn't experienced other cultures or governments, military objectives, or JAGs. Though it was no fault of their own, they had a difficult time understanding what I had been privy to as a result of having had these associations. Their focus was on TV shows, like *Friends* and *The Sopranos*, or baseball games. Whether to buy the latest cell phone and all the other endless stimuli of American pop culture were taking up their energy. I had been away from mainstream American society for four years in service, plus the nine years in medical school and residency. Even though I would still be taking calls and working long hours, this was really the first time I found myself in the drudgery of the nine-to-five office life. I had to debrief myself and relearn everything I had forgotten about being a civilian.

In the midst of all of this, I met a girl. And it was about time: I was thirty-five and still single. Everyone I worked with was married, and my JAG buddies were still in the service and not around to drink Bombay Sapphire Gin with anymore. I met Kari-Ann in Providence on another blind date. We got together in Federal Hill at a well-known fountain in the center. I wanted to at least be on some familiar Little Italy terra firma for this date. Nonetheless, I was still thrown off balance by this attractive, outgoing woman who I knew would fit so perfectly into my family. We dated for about a year while I was in Rhode Island. When my contract came to an end, I was looking to get closer to Pennsylvania. I moved to Maryland, where I started a temporary assignment until I found something more permanent. We continued our relationship from a distance but, at some point, I figured it was time to make things an honest man of myself.

Over Thanksgiving of that year, Kari-Ann came home to Erie with me to experience the circus that was a Rocco Thanksgiving feast. She had met my parents before but had no idea of the band of other personalities she was being thrown into. Papa had passed by then but the rest of the crew would be there. Everyone seemed to be excited to see their prince back in his chair with his princess beside him.

At dinner, I sat in my usual place, on the left side of my father, who was at the head. I was across from Uncle Armand, who was to his right. Kari-Ann was on my left. Following dinner, from the seat I had occupied for so many years, I pulled a ring out of my pocket. I reached down to her left hand, picked it up, and slid the ring onto her fourth finger. I quietly asked if she would marry me, and she said yes! No one witnessed any of this, probably because they were busy arguing over some recent city council controversy. As we sat there looking at each other and the ring, my cousin Tim was the first to realize what had just happened.

"They just got engaged!" he exclaimed.

"What?" my uncle inquired.

"They just got engaged!" Tim repeated.

"When?" Uncle Armand asked.

"*Just now!*" Tim confirmed.

"Are you shitting me?" my father so eloquently expressed.

A whirlwind of activity then followed. Aunt Jill exclaimed, "Weeee!" I guess that can mean happy things, too, depending on the intonation. All the women wanted to see the ring, congratulate and welcome the newest member-to-be of the Rocco family. Aunt B, from her seat of wisdom, pulled Kari-Ann so far into her bosom that she had trouble breathing for a minute or two.

"I got to know your Aunt B and her boobs really well," Kari-Ann later informed me. I told her the diamond on her ring was perfect in that it was exactly one carat, had a colorless D rating, and was internally flawless. I told her it was perfect just like her.

Living apart, we didn't want to waste any time. Four months later, in March, we were married. We went on our honeymoon and three months after that, Kari-Ann was pregnant. Before she delivered, I got an offer from a more permanent practice in Pennsylvania, and we began building a wonderful life for ourselves in Altoona.

During the pregnancy, Kari-Ann asked me if I wanted to try to find my birth mother. She said we could learn more about my medical history for the baby. I told her I didn't want to know.

"What if the baby wants to know?" she asked.

"They won't because they'll know me and I'm healthy," I assured her.

"Shouldn't they know?" she continued.

"Why? I never knew and I turned out fine."

"But what about..."

"No," I cut her off. "I really don't."

I had already flown pretty close to the sun with the aftermath of that first blind date in Philly and didn't like the way the experience affected me emotionally. It left me a crumbled pile of dust for several days and took several weeks to totally get out of my system. Any closer and, you know, Icarus and the wings and all. But Kari-Ann persisted, and this went on for a few months. Then she asked, "Well, if I get the paperwork and fill it out, will you sign it?"

"Sure," I conceded.

I really believed nothing would come of it because I was sure that, after thirty-eight years, my *real* mother would have moved on. She probably had her own family and didn't want to hear from me. Also, I wondered if she ever really existed at all. I knew who I was and rarely ever mentioned the adoption anymore. The courts probably wouldn't release the information anyway, so I'd be safe.

Most importantly, I wasn't worried about finding my mother because I was fixated on meeting my child. Fixated.

My childhood memory of looking for a familiar face in the stores came rushing back. I had forgotten about the insecurity I'd had about physical appearance, and not really looking like anyone in my family and none of them looking like me. Now I was going to meet someone who looked like me — for real. This was going to be an opportunity to finally see myself in another person who I was going to love more than anything in the world.

As a physician, I had delivered a few babies in medical school. I had treated children in school and my own practice, especially during my time at Shriners Hospital. This is the part of being a doctor that sometimes sucks — you know too much. So many things could go wrong during pregnancy. Physicians don't always get credit if things go right, and are considered at least partly responsible if things go wrong. Things are supposed to go right. Doctors spend a lot of time trying to think about all the bad things that can happen before they do and hopefully do something to prevent them, or at least warn the patient.

If you warn the patient of what can go wrong and it happens, you're a genius. If it happens and you didn't warn them, surely you must have done something wrong. When it's your child, you think about *all* the bad things that can happen and more. If you tell your wife those bad things might happen and they do, you are *not* a genius. Your bad thoughts somehow *created* the problem.

Internally, I was a mess. I had heard of women and babies dying in childbirth. My wife didn't have big hips so I worried the baby was going to get stuck and she'd need a C-section. Not to mention, I almost fainted the first time I saw a baby delivered, and that could happen for real this time. My wife was delivering at the hospital where I worked. I didn't want it circulating on the rumor mill that, on the day his wife delivered, Dr. Rocco fainted and peed his pants. So, externally, I prepared to walk into the delivery suite like I owned the place. So, when the time came, I was the picture of calm. That's when you know I'm really scared, when I look as if there isn't a care in the world.

This really pissed Kari-Ann off. As if I wasn't already fully responsible for putting this murderous parasite into her body, now I didn't seem to be worried about it at all. This was no "rush to get to the hospital in a cab" type of trip; I was cool and taking my time.

"No, really, I'm going to have this baby soon!" she told me.

"Okay, let's go. But I have to stop and get some coffee at Sheetz first. A large," I said.

When we arrived, Kari-Ann was a trooper. She got hooked up to the monitors and we started watching the contractions. This was really going to happen. I got calmer, almost in a trance. She got her epidural and wasn't in pain anymore, so I could settle into a book with my coffee and mentally dissociate from the planet until this was all over. I picked a deep, meditative, five-hundred-page book by Jared Diamond called *Collapse*, about the breakdown of civilizations. I'm not sure if I picked the book because it was symbolic of the fact that I thought my life was about to collapse or just because it was the biggest book I had and I thought this was going to take a long time. My wife labored for about an hour and pushed for fifteen minutes before we met our daughter, Sophia. I guess Kari-Ann wasn't kidding. Sophia had been ready to be delivered and my coffee hadn't even cooled long enough for me to enjoy it.

Sophia came out, and they asked if I wanted to cut the umbilical cord. I did, but was more interested in counting her toes and checking her hips to make sure they weren't dislocated. (It's one of the first things you check as an orthopedic surgeon). They cleaned her up and she was fine. APGAR scores of ten and ten; a genius already at birth! Kari-Ann cuddled with her while I stood there confused and dumbfounded, like every other father present at his first child's birth. I knew she was pregnant all along but this was something different. There was an actual baby out here and now she was ours. I was strangely surprised by the reality of it.

Eventually, they let me hold my daughter. As I sat there looking at her closely for the first time, she yawned and I almost died. She yawned just like me. I knew in that instant that she was mine. For the first time in my life, someone else's facial expression became an emotion. It was visceral; I didn't have to think about it. I could empathetically feel it in my gut. I knew what that yawn meant at the mitochondrial level of my soul. I'd seen people yawn for decades and it never affected me the same way. I stared into her eyes while she did it and instantly and without question absorbed the fact that she wasn't even so much mine as she *was* me. Not totally but partly. She was original and unique but there was a large part of her that I could seemingly understand completely. I never experienced that before. That feeling I'd been waiting for since I was a child swept over me. I was holding that familiar person in my hands. I knew without question, without a doubt, that this was my child and my flesh and blood. I was speechless in a way I'd never known.

How could you ever give that away? She didn't look weird at all. She was beautiful!

For the first year, it was ridiculous. Every time she made an expression, I knew what she was feeling. I would joke with my wife at the most awkward times. "That's expression number 1329," I'd say while I was strapping her into her car seat or trying to feed her strained peas. "I know that one!" I'm sure parents do that all the time but, as an adoptee, you don't ever get to experience that in the same way. There is something about your own kind, your own tribe.

Bonding with my daughter brought me so much comfort. I obtained a deeper level of understanding that I believe came straight from my genes. I discovered the part of me that came from my birth parents. She was my first genetic mirror and in her I could see myself. From the thousands of years before me down the line of generations that connects me—from the shape of the nose, the depth of the eyes, and the curve of the eyebrow, down to the soul. It tells you who is a part of you and who you can trust. It also signals who is somewhat different.

My parents loved me and my family fully accepted me, but there was never that same moment of complete and total understanding that I felt for my daughter. It was love of her and selfish love of me. It would not be noble for me to give my life for hers; it would be selfish survival for myself in her. That is what I consider to be unconditional love.

The arrival of my daughter also brought an onslaught of questions for me about nature and nurture. I started thinking about

Journey of the Adopted Self again. Is that deep bond nature or nurture? Does having the experience of bonding with your mother teach you bonding or is it built into the genetic code so that you don't wander away to get eaten by a tiger? Is it a combination of the two in that you inherently have the genes for bonding but bonding is the thing necessary to activate them? If you don't get or lose that early experience, do you become a lone wolf, an opportunist trying to fit in with whomever you happen to encounter? Does it make you a kiss-ass and a con man or have all those charming characteristics needed to help you blend? Maybe it causes you to unnaturally bond with *any* influence in your life and makes you cling to people who end up being bad for you.

Being a mother is an especially awesome thing that I'm very envious of. Your mother is your soil, the ground from which you grew. I have a natural, unforced love and bond with my children, but Kari-Ann's bond with them is even deeper. She carried them in her body for nine months; she fed them milk from her breasts for another year. My son, who was born a few years later, was two and hadn't nursed for over a year, when she got out of the shower. "Mommy, you still have milk in those?" he asked of her breasts. He was so young. How in the world did he remember that?

What was I missing that I never had the chance to experience? Adoptees are often taken from their soil immediately on their first exposure to dry air as a sprout. You would never uproot a plant and move it before establishing firm roots. Why do we feel humans are any different? Did I never develop roots and just learned to suck nutrients from the surface of things as I encountered them? Is that why many adopted children have problems as adults? Did I never experience complete and total bonding and oneness with someone else? Is that something that can't be learned as an adult? Does it only come by experiencing it? Or is it innate in the genes between two genetically related individuals? Do brothers and sisters experience a similar thing? My children seem to have it for one another. Twins seem to have it even stronger. If I had that with my birth mother, would I be better at it today? If I randomly met her on the streets today, would I immediately know?

That experience stirred up more questions in me than answers. I thought about those questions almost every day. Did I have that unselfish love for my friends, my parents, and my wife? Have I ever had that for anyone? Maybe I *was* messed up, as Betty Jean Lifton suspected.

Whatever the reason or cause, I was and still am infinitely grateful for experiencing it with my children. Having been on the outside of that relationship as an adoptee, the whole process is so unbelievably natural and mysterious and beautiful and irreplaceable to me. It has added so much to the development of my current understanding of myself, my children, Kari-Ann, and mothers and babies everywhere.

Soon after Sophia's first birthday, we bought a gorgeous four-bedroom brick and stucco house on top of a hill that gave us a nearly 360-degree view of the town below and the Pennsylvania mountains beyond it. From this perch, on the Fourth of July we could easily count ten different fireworks displays in every direction. Our nearest neighbor was more than a quarter of a mile away, and we were surrounded by 118 acres of field and forest that we called our own. Instead of the plum, pear, and walnut trees that circled my Papa's house, we had red and white oak trees, cherry trees, and a good deal of mountain laurel. In addition to wasp nests, we had herds of deer and flocks of turkeys in the field, along with coyotes, bobcats, and the occasional black bear strolling through our backyard. Papa would have loved it.

We had family reunions at the house and spent a good deal of time on ATVs and shooting clay pigeons with my new shotgun in the field across the way. I never shot a gun in the military but now I was trying my damnedest to immerse myself in all this good old country, central Pennsylvania so-called redneck fun.

The driveway up to the house from the main road was three tenths of a mile long and very steep, which made for a number of difficult drives up- or downhill in the middle of winter. On more than a few occasions, our cars would begin sliding down the hill on the ice and then spin into a very nice pirouette as our views changed from looking down the hill, to up the hill, to back down again. Our asses would bite deeply into the car seat until we came to a stop. Most of the time we could then pull out from a flat spot at the bottom. On occasion, I would have to get out the ninety-one-horsepower John Deere tractor to pull the car out of the field. That tractor was a true savior for our family and neighbors.

Given that we didn't have any immediate family in the area and that I was often on call, we were typically invited to the neighbors' holiday parties and often got together for neighborhood events and annual picnics. My neighbors were a close-knit group and had all known each other well for generations.

Over the next two years, first smiles, words, steps, diaper changes, and broken rest consumed our days. I had long forgotten about signing the paperwork to receive my adoption information, but almost three years after putting pen to paper, I received a call from a representative with the state. I was driving home from work and returned a voice mail. It was a brief call and the woman explained that they had just picked up my file and had some leads. I was uncharacteristically quiet and didn't even mention the call to Kari-Ann. I was secretly hoping it wouldn't work out. Three days later, the woman called back and said she had found my mother, who was comfortable with me contacting her. She gave me her phone number, her email, and her name: Joyce.

This moment wasn't like the child's fantasy moment I had imagined innumerable times growing up. There was no tear-jerking music in the background. No camera zooming in for a close-up of my widening eyes as the reality of it all set in. The normalness of it was probably the thing that made it all the stranger. "Okay, we found your mother, here's her info." That's it? Don't I need a counselor here with me or something?

The representative said she would send me a package with my original birth certificate, some identifying information on my mother, and a transcript from the court proceedings where she signed me away. Oh, and there was one more thing. She said that at least one of my parents was African-American.

That little side note honestly didn't surprise me in the least. Somehow it was like I knew all along. I just knew, and my heart didn't slow down or speed up one beat with this information. I had just found my mother! I was in too much shock over that to get into the details of my racial blend. Almost as soon as the words "African-American" hit my eardrums, my deep subconscious brain replied, "Yeah, we knew that."

Arriving home fifteen minutes later, I googled Joyce and found she had a huge website as a historian and genealogist, with thousands of pages on her local area, about three hours away from us. She posted about historic events and family interest stories. On her homepage was a silhouette of herself, a Caucasian woman, and her eyes were immediately familiar to me as my own. On the page entitled *My Family Tree*, it listed her, her parents, and over ten generations dating back to the 1400s. There was even a brief journey on the Mayflower in 1620. How cool! She didn't list any children. She had a photo of herself on the family tree section from when she was four or five. This photo looked unbelievably like my daughter, who was a little over two at the time.

I couldn't help being a little disappointed that all the research leading to these thousands of pages of text never once mentioned the child she carried in her womb for nine months and delivered more than forty years ago. I understood. I knew she remembered me, but wasn't surprised in the least that she couldn't put that out there for public consumption. Discovering this large amount of information so quickly was overwhelming. The steel door was instantly unlocked and, as I peered in, I saw a long hallway that seemed to go on forever. I was amazed that my being had started long before my parents got me. Holy shit! I had a real past. I didn't just pop onto the planet under that desert rock my family always joked about.

I devoured her website and was amazed and kind of proud that I was loosely tied to the founding of our nation. The next day,

I went to a quiet corner of our backyard to call Joyce on my cell phone. It was a 570 area code, from a part of the state I thought I had never been to. This time, as opposed to the awkward wrong-number message I received in Philly, I had an actual vision of my birth mother from her website. I knew immediately she was the real deal.

I dialed the number and she quickly picked up and said, "Hello."

"Hi, is this Joyce?" I asked.

"Yes," she replied.

"Hello, this is Jack," I told her.

"Hello, Jack," she excitedly replied. "I've been hoping to hear from you."

"I know. It's been a while, huh?" I cutely threw in.

She said she thought about me frequently but knew I had to be the one to initiate the search. I tried to fill her in on the past forty-one years. I told her about my family, my schooling, my career, and the fact that she had a granddaughter.

She told me about her life and her career and how, following my birth, her life went on a slight detour. She worked as a waitress until she eventually married and went back to school, but never had any other children.

Her story was similar to what I had been told. She was in college and somewhat poor for a student. She met a young man and got pregnant. I didn't push her on the details but she made it clear that it was a brief relationship. She had two photos of my father and offered to email them to me. One was his senior photo and the other was from the yearbook, with the two of them together. His name was Larry. I instantly remembered my parents telling me the nuns called me Larry. All this time we thought the nuns made it up, but it was Joyce who actually gave me my birth father's name.

I can't explain why I didn't put two and two together and figure that out ages ago. She told me that Larry had a darker complexion but was very light-skinned. He could've easily been

Italian or Middle Eastern. She said some of her friends thought he might have been part Black but some didn't suspect at all. He was mixed. Either way, I did look a hell of a lot like him in the photos she sent. Joyce told me that after being contacted by the state she searched for him and found an obituary revealing that Larry had passed away about a year earlier.

There was an unexpected ease to the conversation that only two people with the same secret experience could ever have. There was no need to spruce it up or try and impress. It was an attempt at complete and total honesty, as if we each didn't want to misrepresent any of our words or feelings for fear of giving incorrect information. It was as if I knew she would know if I was lying. I was astonished by how so many components of our conversation were effortless; she said things that were very similar to things I had said before. From our beliefs on religion and our skepticism of the system to our approach to problem-solving and intellectual curiosity, I could recognize a manner of thinking that was very much like my own. There was a lot of "Yeah, right?" and "I know what you're saying!" without having to ask clarifying questions.

It wasn't until then that I realized it did kind of suck not knowing why I was the way I was all these years; why I couldn't just accept me as me. "Well, that's just Jack. He's a little different," my family and friends seemed to unintentionally imply with subconscious expressions. I quickly recognized that I had been reading those subtle implications from a very early age all along. I *was* different. The thing is, I wasn't that much different from Joyce. I wasted a lot of time trying to deny myself or feeling weird for being the way I was. I recognized for the first time that I may have spent a great deal of my life blending, conforming, and camouflaging myself. I didn't know any better, so I wasted a lot of energy trying to build or justify my worth not just accepting how I was as a natural gift.

Fortunately, my parents truly did just let me be, for the most part. In retrospect, I have to say they really did a great job of staying out of my way. I didn't know them when we met and they had no idea what they had with me either. I was a complete mystery to both them and myself as I developed. My stubborn assertiveness seemed to be a characteristic I may have received from Joyce as well. Had I been more reserved, perhaps I would have been less insistent and just blindly complied without question. Who knows?

Joyce and I eventually agreed to continue with emails and did so for several months before we met face-to-face. Even by email, it was unusual to have so much agreement and understanding with someone I had never met. I thought I was just quirkily original, but she was definitely my compatriot.

Eventually I received the information from the state, including a transcript of the court proceedings. Within the first few sentences the judge asked Joyce, "Are you the mother of this Negro Child?"

"Negro child?" I thought. "I'm not a Negro child." How did the judge know Larry was Black if Joyce wasn't sure? She didn't really know much about him besides what you could see in the black-and-white photo. We estimated him to be maybe one-eighth Black at most.

This court document was from 1966, and sadly (or fortunately) I honestly wasn't aware there was such racial discrimination at that time. It was especially strange to me that a judge would use the term "Negro Child" in court. This wasn't the deep south, this was Erie, Pennsylvania. But this was also the civil rights era. I'm sure people were paying attention and he apparently didn't look "that Black." Maybe he could still be at least part Italian. Why does it even matter? Clearly the judge was trying to embarrass or belittle Joyce even further.

Was I really part Black? I mentioned that it was something that I subconsciously seemed to just know, but why? What was it? Slowly at first but then increasingly, the waterfall of evidence from my past memories began bursting through the dam that the closed adoption system had held in place for so many years. Looking back at my past, many people called me out on those stereotypes all along. I always did have thick, dark, kinky hair, which my friends frequently referred to as a Brillo pad. One friend even told me in front of our crew that my hair was like a Play Doh Fuzzy Pumper. Other classmates who knew I was adopted joked over the years that I might be Black because they said I had a "bubble butt," was a "good dancer," or "had some speed." I tried to not let it bother me, but I really didn't like that attention. Being the only white guy on the all-Black relay team in high school probably wasn't such an aberration after all.

It was odd, but I wasn't even slightly surprised. By that time, I think I somehow deeply knew this was the case even though I never allowed myself to acknowledge it. Of course, I never told myself any of that because I wasn't allowed to tell myself that. Up until then, I was a white doctor named Jack. Up until then, I was the Italian kid from a blue-collar family who worked his way through the many layers of higher education. Up until then, I was the prince who got upset if his peas got mixed in with his mashed potatoes on the plate. Meeting this one key person, my birth mother, instantly changed my identity with that pesky little thing called the truth.

Prior to finding Joyce, the adoption fog and denial I was in was so thick. As Pandora's box opened, parts of the real me were emerging. I was curious what I was going to find next but also somewhat tentative and paralyzed with fear. I felt I had to be careful to not completely unwind the knot that had bound me so nicely into the guy I thought I knew as Jack. I sensed that unraveling it too fast might just cause me to suddenly fall into a heap of unrecognizable meaningless slime on the floor. The very bones and foundation holding me up were coming into question.

I was trying to efficiently and accurately reassemble these new parts. Who was this man I now looked at in the mirror? I had no idea, but at least I had some better clues to start figuring out the mystery.

Eventually, Kari-Ann, Sophia, and I drove to meet Joyce and learn more about her story. It didn't deviate much from what my parents had been told all along. Joyce had a lot of stories about her family, her parents, and life growing up in north central Pennsylvania. She was predominantly English and had a photo of her father, who did this thing with his eyebrows that I can also do. As she told me about her lineage, coming from a line of settlers tied to the Mayflower, I also felt uneasy. My immigrant story and identity were slowly slipping away or being watered down. The blue-collar origin story was being chipped away by this story of American insider privilege.

Joyce told me so many tales about my grandfather, grandmother, and aunts and uncles. It was all very interesting, but none of it felt like my family. I was realizing they were family, but I didn't really want to erase all the aunts and uncles I already had and put these new ones in their place. I had my story and was somewhat resistant to have to learn another one.

Joyce also shared the ordeal she went through once she suspected she was pregnant. She went to the doctor, who confirmed it, and then she had to figure out what to do. In the sixties, many people in that situation got married. She walked down Main Street in Mansfield, Pennsylvania, from her doctor's appointment to the football field where Larry was practicing. She told him she was pregnant, and marriage apparently wasn't an option. Once she started to look pregnant, she went away to "visit an aunt" until she could deliver.

I later read *The Girls Who Went Away* by Ann Fessler, which gives an incredible account of the traumatic events and emotions these women went through. They were often coerced or downright forced by their parents, doctors, and priests to give these children over to an agency so "good families" could raise them.

Joyce's story had a reasonably happy ending. After delivering me, her career as a teacher was derailed, and she worked as a waitress for a summer then got back into teaching for a couple of years. She went on to graduate school, became an accountant, and got married, but didn't want children. When her husband passed away, she immersed herself in her career and academic interests until she retired and moved back onto her parents' farm. That explained why it was so easy to locate her. Her address was the same as it had been in 1966. These days she was founder of a local history center and writing various articles about her community. It was a relatively nice, benign story without a lot of unexpected drama, poverty, or violence. Something I could easily digest.

In our meeting, I realized and found it interesting that all these years, while I had no past, Joyce, having no children in her life, seemed to have no future. That similarity, albeit polarized, served as a stark contrast in our perspectives which seemed to have affected our personalities as well. I was always looking to the future in my life, while she seemed to be looking into the past with her role as a historian, genealogist, and museum curator. Our meeting seemed to complete each of us somewhat, in that it allowed her to see her future in me and my children while I was simultaneously recognizing my past in her. Profound.

Unfortunately, there were also things about Joyce that I didn't like. It wasn't anything major, but I soon realized she had a number of characteristics I recognized as things about myself. I could empathize with my critics more than I felt comfortable admitting at the time. Carl Jung said, "Everything that irritates us about others can lead us to an understanding of ourselves." This is especially true about our parents. It was only after meeting and learning about Joyce that I thought, *Oh yeah, I get why I can be annoying sometimes,* and *Yeah, I am kind of a nerd.* Even though it was a tough pill to swallow, I was also mischievously giggling inside that I now finally had a fellow like-minded nerd who was mine.

My orphanage story really wasn't that bad, tragic, or different from the story I had been told. The nuns were safe for now and back in the good-guys column. Sure, they didn't tell me that Larry was my birth father's name, but, hell, maybe they didn't know. Right? Maybe? They might have made up the part about me being Italian for my parents' benefit. Larry might still be Italian...and Black.

Joyce and I maintained a somewhat clandestine relationship,

meeting once or twice a year at her house or mine. I got to hear all her stories and share ours. It was great for her to meet her grandchildren and for them to meet her. They didn't know she was their grandmother initially because I hadn't told my parents any of this. I didn't want my children to accidentally spill the beans to my parents, so we told them Joyce was just one of Daddy's friends from college.

I did share all of this with my sister Lisa, and she was a huge help to me as I processed everything. She was the only person in the world I felt comfortable going to about this at the time. She understood and shared in my battling emotions and concerns.

Finding Joyce made me feel somewhat more comfortable in my own skin. Starting to grasp that two actual human beings conceived me, a mother carried me for nine months, and I had an actual birthday — not just a Gotday — was comforting. It's weird, but I really never honestly realized anything like that happened to me.

After finding Joyce, I would often walk by a mirror, see my reflection, and stop to look deep into my own eyes. I would stare at my facial features and my skin. For the first time, I was searching for someone else within my characteristics. Having blocked out the possibility of being anything other than an Italian working-class guy for years, I struggled to tie these new truths to my internal vision of myself. I couldn't do it. Who I looked at in the mirror and who I now knew myself to be — or thought I was previously — wouldn't connect in my mind as the same person.

What's more, I realized that I wasn't ever a *tabula rasa*, or blank slate, when my parents got me. I had some of Joyce's tendencies and nature in me all along. Then my parents filled in teachings needed to nurture and make me who I was.

I also concluded at the time that even though Joyce gave me away, she really did the best thing any human could do for another human. She gave me life. And she gave me freedom. It was ultimate freedom in that, other than my genetic makeup, she didn't influence the early me, through nurture, one bit. I loved my family but somehow always knew and felt I was somewhat different. Everyone in my family was very proud of me but also kind of surprised and amazed as well. So who was I? As a young child, I would have never imagined becoming a doctor — let alone a surgeon. Many things made more sense to me now. I had some genetic inclination for academics and a perfect environment in which to thrive.

Had Joyce and Larry raised me, I may have been encouraged to do something my biological father, mother, or grandparents did. There may have been some expectation for success, and I would have had a yard marker or goal of sorts to achieve in order to be judged as successful. In my family, there were no specific expectations of me. Almost every day something new could pop up out of nowhere and none of us could predict what would happen next. I had freedom to chase my American dream and I somehow exceeded everyone's hopes.

There was still the mystery of my birth father, but I'd had enough at the time. I wasn't ready to poke at that wasp's nest again. Not yet.

CHAPTER 7
PERFECT LIFE

"WHO KNEW?" MY WIFE REMARKED TO ME. "I THOUGHT I WAS marrying a white doctor named Jack. It turns out I married a Black farmer named Larry." She had a point. Imagine my surprise.

Driving to work or sitting in my tractor brush hogging the field, I would often catch myself daydreaming about this past life that was locked behind that steel door constructed after my birth. Growing up, I just went along with what I was told. It was now embarrassingly obvious to me. Was it obvious to everyone else as well? Was I the only one not in on the joke? What would have happened if I had been allowed to be that original child? There were seemingly two mes: the one who I was and the one who I should have been. How would he have turned out? Would he have been an orthopedic surgeon, Italian, Catholic, Democrat, and a Yankees fan?

Adoptees are typically aware of the duality of their lives, always wondering about the version of themselves that never was. For me, it was as though there's a vanishing twin that was lost at birth before I went on to become the chosen one, the special child. That twin of mine would have certainly been special in 1966, being a part Black child born out of wedlock to a single mother. How would he have fared in life?

We didn't know what Larry's racial makeup was. But just like the judge at Joyce's court appearance, it seemed I somehow knew or could feel that I had Black heritage myself all along. In a way, I felt complicit in the lie, in that my heart and soul had been telling me that for years and I just never heard them, at times, screaming at me.

While I began thinking about who I was much more deeply, I also began to consider *real kids* more deeply as well: kids who knew and never questioned their parents their whole lives. How did that affect them? They *never* think to question their identity and really have no reason to. They often just carry on with their one unexamined existence. Having only one view of the world leaves them free of the nonstop mental twister game I was playing in my head. In a way I felt a little sad for them. I had just found one of my parents and suddenly it seemed as though I—and others —had to reconsider who I was.

I wasn't sure if I could tell everyone about my discovery. When I mentioned my newly discovered background to my Black friends, it was often met with enthusiasm and excitement. "That's awesome, man! My brother from another mother! Welcome," said Zane Gates, MD, a local family practice colleague and friend. Revealing this fact to white friends, however, was sometimes met with more of an uncomfortable silence or canned reassurance that it didn't really matter. There was a sense that because they said, "it doesn't matter," that it somehow did matter.

Then there was John Lehman, my best friend in residency and best man at my wedding. When I told him that I found out I was part Black, I was surprised by his lack of surprise.

"No shit, Jack!" he said instantly in knee-jerk reaction. "I could have guessed that."

It didn't take me long to realize this was true.

"And then there was…" but he quickly stopped himself because my wife was present at the time.

He rightly figured that she didn't know I had dated a few Black women back in the day. Almost no one knew that except for John and his wife, Angie.

I dated a few women of color during residency and got along great with them. Unfortunately, at the time (possibly due to my adopted personality and inclination to not rock the boat), I never invited them to the department functions. I usually went alone or brought a white girl who could blend into the background with me and not bring me any unwanted attention. I didn't want attention. Given that I already felt as if I'd snuck into the orthopedic department, I preferred to blend into the wallpaper.

I wasn't wrong about African Americans standing out in this crowd. Orthopedics is notoriously one of the least diverse medical specialties in the country. Female orthopedists are uncommon but increasing. Black orthopedists are rare. African Americans make up only about 4 percent of those entering residency classes and 1.5 percent of all orthopedists. Temple actually had three during my years in training and that wasn't bad. One of our Black residents at Temple refused to go to our annual alumni event every year because it was held at a country club where Blacks were prohibited from joining. Even though some of the other residents rolled their eyes at his boycott, I thought he had some *cojones* for taking a stand like that. I wasn't that brave. Turns out, he probably had an impact. By my senior year, the event was moved to another club.

Now I was ashamed by that external denial of my internal preferences. What if I had known of my heritage and racial blend earlier in life? Would I have been less insecure about who I was dating? There was no way to know but I definitely felt even worse about those facts now that I knew I shared a part of my race with them. Mine was just legally erased. I guess it was a blessing and a curse that I didn't look Black. Sarcasm intended.

This newfound identity was on my mind a lot after meeting Joyce, but I didn't really know what to do about it. Life had to go on. I was now in one of the largest private practice orthopedic groups in central Pennsylvania and the pace of work fast and the competition between the partners was palpable. I was doing well in the practice and consistently right in the middle of the pack of income producers. In a private practice, it's widely known that income productivity is clearly the best method for judging your effectiveness as a physician. (Sarcasm intended, once again.) Often the highest producers were somewhat suspect narcissistic egomaniacs and the low producers were just bad or lazy — or both. I was in the middle, so I was normal. Kind of.

Eventually I left my private practice for a hospital owned group and my career grew even further. Now I was treating a good number of the hospital staff, administrators, and board members as well. We were invited to all the hospital-based galas and fundraising events, even holding one in front of our house to highlight our beautiful view of the surrounding area. We were living large.

Soon after moving to Altoona, I also joined the Freemasons and Shriners International. Given the deep respect for the organization we had as a family, I felt obligated to pay back and support the group. Many of America's founding fathers, like George Washington and Ben Franklin, were Freemasons. The Shriners International organization is essentially the philanthropic and social arm of the Freemasons. The Shriners hospitals (like the one where my Aunt B went for her recovery) were formed in the 1920s as a philanthropic endeavor to help with the polio outbreak.

Altoona has a very active and thriving Masonic and Shriner organization with a lot of influential members. I donned my red fez proudly every time I went to gatherings. After a few years, my peers in the group nominated me to be on the Board of Governors as their representative in Philadelphia. To be able to return to Philly, where I did my residency, as a member of the Board of Governors was one of the biggest honors of my life. I'm still surprised that Aunt B didn't come back from her grave to swear me in at the ceremony. She would have absolutely busted her buttons to have seen that.

Around that same time, we also started our own nonprofit

organization. In mid to late July 2010 during a steak dinner at my house, some friends and I got into a discussion over some beers in the garage. My friend Wes had recently traveled to Madagascar on a mission trip with an optometrist friend of ours to provide eyeglasses. "If you ever go back, let me know. I'd love to go," I told him. Three weeks later, I got a text message saying, "Hey, I talked to Aaron, and he would love for you to run an orthopedic mission in the bush."

My first reaction to his text was, *I should have kept my big mouth shut*. I knew absolutely nothing about running orthopedic missions in the bush. When I'd mentioned it to him, I was just hoping to be able to carry some boxes of glasses. I briefly mentioned this to Carla, a nurse I worked with in the OR. "That's great," she said. "You should do it. I'd love to do something like that." Jen, my scrub tech at the time, agreed that she'd love to go as well. "We should all go," Carla exclaimed. Next thing you know we're trying to organize a group of our colleagues to go on a medical mission trip to Madagascar.

By the beginning of September, we had our first group meeting at my house. The goal was to convince Brian, a nurse anesthetist we worked with, to join us. We knew we had to butter up his wife, Jill, also a nurse, in order for him to be allowed to go. She quickly got swept up in the excitement and wanted to come along as well. That's how easily the team came together and in less than six weeks. It was made up of Kari-Ann, Carla Baldessaro, Jen Miller, Brian and Jill Duclos, Wes Reed, and me. Wes, of course, because he started this whole ridiculous idea, eventually had to bail. He ended up developing a blood clot in his leg. He wasn't really excited to go back in the first place, after suffering through the hardship of overseas travel, so we joked with him that we think he may have faked it. Justin Kurpeikis, his coworker and a former Penn State and NFL football player, quickly took Wes's place. We were glad to have him on board for his orthopedic knowledge as well as his massive size, which made him a great bodyguard.

At that early September meeting, we decided we needed to

have a fundraiser to help with the costs of our trip. We called ourselves Operation Small Steps, or OSS. The name was a reference to the small feet of the children we were planning to help, but also to taking a small step to make the world a better place. On October 2, we held our first fundraising event in my backyard, which we cleverly named Rocctoberfest. Less than four weeks after assembling our team, we managed to put together an event with three hundred people, five bands, four tents, food, beer, wine, and prizes; we raised approximately fifteen thousand dollars. As we tallied up our proceeds, we realized this was now a real endeavor and, after taking everyone's money, there was no turning back. The trip was slated for April 2011.

For the next several months, we did more fundraising, collected donated equipment, and tried to anticipate and train for the type of conditions we would encounter. I educated the team and we adopted my Air Force philosophy of Semper Gumby, as no amount of training could prepare us for the experience of being on the ground in Antananarivo, the capital of Madagascar. Then we all packed our bags and supplies, got on a plane, and headed out on our mission.

Door to hotel-room door, the voyage to this island country off the southeast coast of Africa lasted thirty-three hours. It was after midnight when we checked into our hotel. Everything was dark and rushed and crowded and we couldn't really see much. After a day and a half of travel, we were all confused, dead tired, and slept like babies. The following morning was incredibly disorienting, waking up and looking around the room. Where the hell were we?

I got out of bed and looked out the window. This looked nothing like the Dreamworks movie. There were no penguins at all, just the red clay which can frequently be seen along its many dusty dirt roads, homes, and fields. I saw crowded, open street markets with raw meat hanging in the heat of the shop windows and people with brightly colored clothing. I turned to Kari-Ann and said, "Holy cow, we're in Madagascar!"

Madagascar is unique in that it has a mix of influences from both Africa and Indonesia. The native language is Malagasy, but there is also a primary influence of French from the time when it was a French colony. Many of its early Indonesian settlers ventured around the Indian Ocean on outrigger canoes similar to those used by the inhabitants of Hawaii. It is known for its unique flora and fauna, like bandit-eyed lemurs. Just as on the Galapagos Islands, they evolved independent of the mainland for millions of years.

Everything was different from what I'd experienced at home and while in the service—especially the poverty. Madagascar is incredibly beautiful and exotic in places but also very dirty, foul-smelling, and impoverished in others. It's one of the world's poorest nations.

Upon arriving in the country, we met our hosts, Aaron and Heather Santmyier. They were on a three-year mission with the Assemblies of God national churches and had been involved in mission work for a good part of their adult lives. Heather grew up overseas in the mission field and Aaron used his doctorate in nursing to deliver all varieties of medical care out of his mobile clinic.

Heather also ran an orphanage in Antananarivo while Aaron was away in the bush or rainforest on one of his outreach missions. Within a day or two of our arrival, Heather brought us to tour her orphanage. This was the first of many orphanages I would find myself in since my brief stay at the St. Joseph's Orphanage in Erie forty-five years earlier.

During each of our subsequent trips, we routinely visited a number of schools and orphanages to talk to the children and raise awareness of our mission, which eventually morphed primarily into treating clubfoot. When we first arrived, we had no idea what we would focus on. Then we saw how rampant clubfoot was and realized this was where we could most effectively focus our work.

Clubfoot is a relatively common condition experienced all

around the world. It occurs in one to eight out of every one thousand births, with the vast majority occurring in low-income countries. In the US, it is commonly treated with serial castings, which can dramatically improve the function of the patient to near normalcy in the long run. Unfortunately, in many underdeveloped countries, it often goes untreated and can progress to much more severe deformities, with the patient walking on the outside portion of the ankle and the sole of the foot pointing backwards. Often the deformity progresses to the point where, as an adult, they can no longer walk and many are forced to crawl around on all fours.

As we drove through the gates to her orphanage, Heather commented that she was upset with the workers because they were taking too long raising the height of the wall surrounding the compound. The top of the brick wall was capped in concrete, with thousands of shards of broken glass embedded in it to act as a makeshift razor wire. There had been a few break-ins recently, she explained, and they thought raising the height of the wall would help.

When I think back to those trips, the sight of that wall stands out so significantly. The concerns we had for the safety of our food and water, the risk of malaria, the filthiness of the operating rooms and living quarters we were exposed to—all of it paled in comparison to the dangers symbolized in that wall. That broken-glass-topped wall has become an emblem of what I believe is one of the most significant human dangers and injustice in Madagascar and the world.

As we toured the very sparse and humble facilities and dorm-style bedrooms of the orphanage, Justin questioned the break-ins. "What would anyone possibly want to steal from here?" he asked.

"The girls," Heather quickly informed us.

That possibility had never even crossed my mind, and the brutal reality struck me as we stood in silence, realizing that the evils of human trafficking were all around us — and, specifically, just on the other side of that wall.

My suffering and identity issues were nothing compared to

what some of these children had to deal with. I never once considered that being put up for adoption would put me at risk of being sold into the sex or drug trade. Why in the hell was I whining about not knowing my birth parents?

No matter where I turned — America, Japan, Madagascar — there were always very good people trying to rectify the evils of the world. One of the biggest dangers and often-ignored realities of the world is having unwanted children. The lies, shame, and cover-ups around it only add to the complexity of the problem. Most of us engage in and are the result of some type of a sexual act. However, when this act results in an unwanted child, it becomes a big problem.

Humans have historically battled big problems with many creative solutions. But then again, there are always those who will exploit this problem for their own benefit. These "evil" humans, like the crack dealers I encountered during my residency, were unfortunately often just trying to get by in a very messed-up world themselves. They may have been unwanted or abandoned themselves and were put in a situation where they almost *had* to be "evil" just to survive. The cycle has been occurring for millennia and individuals seem to *choose* their side of the wall. Or do they? Perhaps it was just terrible luck regarding which side they found themselves on before they could even make an informed decision. Those stolen children could easily become the world's next child stealers.

Aaron and Heather arranged our bush experience at a clinic in Mandritsara run by Adrien Ralaimiarison. If Antananarivo looked poor and exploited, Mandritsara looked like a scene out of a Bible movie—but with a modern twist. We saw clay and straw-built homes lining deeply weathered and eroded streets; dozens of oxen being herded through the village; children playing in the streets or just sitting in the dirt, often with no sign of adults around. We also witnessed women and children bathing and washing clothes in the same stream where men were washing their motorcycles. I'd see the occasional guy talking on a cell phone in a dusty field where a freshly slaughtered zebu (ox) was hanging from a nearby tree. It was surreal. We laughed because when we arrived in Madagascar, Antananarivo was the poorest scene we had ever seen. After being in Mandritsara and returning to the capital, it was like a breath of fresh air to be back in civilization.

Dr. Adrien lived within the hospital compound with his wife, Giselle, and their family. He functioned as the hospital's physician and surgeon, in addition to being its pastor, boss, and surrogate father. Watching him be so compassionate and stern or kind and strict in equal measure, I witnessed a perfect balance of expression that I'd never seen from anyone before or since. He has since passed, and the world is infinitely worse off for the loss of this great man.

Following a morning prayer service led by Dr. Adrien, where he introduced our team, we made our way to the clinic. The first patient was walking in front of me as we slowly traversed the walkway. She was a seven-year-old who had severe bilateral clubfeet. As she progressed toward our new clinic, her flimsy blue flip-flops were aligned in a north-south direction. Unfortunately, her clubfeet were simultaneously aligned in an east-west direction. In a strange island country almost nine thousand miles from my home, I walked behind her silently, petrified.

What was I supposed to do with this? I knew the procedure necessary to realign her feet and had assisted on some during my time at Shriners, but was I able to accomplish it here, at this time? The pressure to magically save all the sad and deformed patients coming to see us was intense. The hospital had a radio station, which had announced our arrival for weeks in advance. Some of these patients walked for four days to come see us. We clearly couldn't treat them all, but as I examined this first patient, I had to somehow stall before I could commit to anything. What else were we expected to do this week that I hadn't even seen yet?

My decision was soon made for me, about a dozen patients later, when I met Felix. He was seventeen years old and also had bilateral clubfeet, which were worse than that first patient because of the added years of neglect. His right foot had been partially corrected five years earlier by the last orthopedic surgeon to visit this remote hospital. They wanted me to correct his left foot to match the right one. Felix was an orphan who had recently converted to Christianity, and was Dr. Adrien's favorite patient.

"Please, Jack, please, can you fix Felix?" Dr. Adrien implored.

I didn't feel like I had a choice. We had traveled halfway across the world to get here. No other orthopedic surgeon had visited this town in five years and, for some godforsaken reason, I was brought here to do who knew what. I conferred with my team-mates later in the day.

"Jen, do we have the equipment to do this procedure?" I asked.

"I don't know, what do you need?" she replied.

I went over the procedure with her and we thought through what we would need. "Brian, can we do his anesthesia here?" I asked.

"Yeah, I think we can. It's not the same equipment we have at home but they do anesthesia here all the time. We should be okay," he replied.

"Carla, what do you think? Can we do this?"

"That's up to you, Jack," she said. "What do you think?" She was right, it was up to me—but I didn't know what to think.

We had a binder of articles and procedures to review from other mission trips and clubfoot programs established in Uganda years earlier by Norgrove Penny, a well-known orthopedic surgeon from British Columbia. While I'd assisted in several club-foot procedures at Shriners Hospital in Philadelphia, none of them were this bad. Since that time, I had become much more confident with my orthopedic skills after four years of flying solo in Japan and ten years in private practice, but could anyone correct a foot this bad? His right foot wasn't perfect either, but it was better than his left, and Felix was happy with it. He only wanted the left foot to match the right so he could ride a bike instead of walking around on crutches all the time.

I looked through the articles and thought carefully about what

to do. We had raised tens of thousands of dollars and spent countless hours preparing for this trip. I had lived my entire life
preparing for this moment and forces in the universe had
somehow placed me here, at this time, under this pressure, for
some reason.

I decided we had to do it. It was a go, but I needed to acquire
some easier experience first before working on Felix. I would start
with that first patient, who had a relatively mild impairment, and
then progress to a second young man I had seen earlier before
operating on Felix.

The so-called operating rooms were housed within a cinder-
block-and-brick building which was very much open to the
outside air — including open widows. We actually had to run
around trying to catch a grasshopper who entered the OR without
authorization before starting an operation one day. It was normal
for there to be a staff member assigned to the room with a fly
swatter in hand, which he frequently used.

Despite the conditions, the procedures, including Felix's, all
went well, without any complications, and the corrections
improved the alignment of all the horribly deformed feet we saw.
The patients were uncomfortable postoperatively, of course, especially given that the only pain reliever available to us was IV aceta-
minophen (Tylenol). Dr. Adrien, the patients, and their families
were all very happy with the work we had done. It was a level of
medical care above anything else they had ever received in this
town before.

Initially we thought our trip to Madagascar would be a one-
and-done journey. But when we realized the impact we were able
to have and got to sit in the joy of pulling off such a life-changing
experience for so many patients, we knew we had to go back. After
that first trip to Madagascar, I went to some training courses and
actually met Norgrove Penny, whose articles I'd relied on so
heavily during the visit to Madagascar. Norgrove was on the board
of Christian Blind Mission. I told him of the trip we made to Madagascar and he said something to the effect of, "No one thinks much

about Madagascar." He knew how overlooked it was when doctors were considering medical missions to Africa.

Over the next year he put me in touch with Steve Manion, MD, another orthopedic surgeon from England who was working with CBM. We coordinated our next trip the following year to coincide with a trip CBM organized. We were able to work together and help put them in contact with some of the same organizations we worked with. We worked side by side in Antananarivo for two days that year, learning from them as well as sharing some of the experiences we'd had in the country. They also joined us for a Rotary Club meeting in the capital to promote both of our organizations. They have continued to organize trips there and I was proud of the role we played in introducing the country and the opportunity to them.

That second year, we also returned to Mandritsara and were able to see more patients and do more surgeries with the help of Eric Shirley, MD, a pediatric orthopedic surgeon from Jacksonville, Florida. On that second trip, we focused primarily on clubfoot, as that seemed to be the problem we could most effectively treat. The volume of cases was overwhelming but we did the best we could. Fred Khaloff, DO, an anesthesiologist we knew from Altoona, and his daughter, Natalie, joined the team as well and performed spinal epidural blocks on patients, including a pregnant mother, to help with pain control. The mother delivered her beautiful new baby daughter comfortably and honored us by naming her Kari-Ann.

John Roberts, a local orthotist, came along as well, since brace-making was an integral part of the treatment. He taught the staff, along with a shoemaker in the region, how to make braces for the children. Over the years we also brought with us a number of nurses and nursing students from Penn State University to help.

Justin came again the second year and kept us safe and in constant tears laughing our asses off with his tremendous sense of humor. The organization was growing and receiving tremendous local support.

We did a total of four trips in a six-year period. Each of the first two trips allowed us to operate on thirty patients and see 150 patients each year. The volume of cases was overwhelming, but we managed to gain a fair amount of notoriety for our efforts and passion. We realized that surgery was not a sustainable solution, given the infrastructure of the country and its inherent risk. During the last two missions, we moved from doing surgeries to teaching casting techniques, especially for younger children, for whom the treatment can actually be relatively curative. Local rheumatologist Fred Murphy, DO, and his daughter, Kaitlyn, came with us and helped organize educational programs for the technique. It was something which could be further taught throughout the country, where surgical suites and qualified individuals were essentially nonexistent. The casting treatment still posed many challenges to the locals, but it was a much more sustainable treatment method for that country.

The team had further matured in efficiency by the time we began to partner with a new friend from nearby State College, Sandratra Kerr, and her organization Echoes of Madagascar. She joined us on our last two trips and helped with our local fundrais- ers. She was able to connect us with an unbelievable amount of local Malagasy talent and resources. We were subsequently able to meet with many local government officials at the national level. Her organization continues to visit and assist the country in many important ways to this day.

As we switched to more teaching of the casting technique, we were able to educate over a hundred physicians, technicians, and nurses each year. One physician spent four days walking and hitchhiking from the rain forest region to attend our lectures. During our final trip we went back to his village specifically to further train him and his staff. We held a fantastic one-day seminar where we educated the patients and families, met with local government representatives, and casted between fifty and sixty patients. We felt our presence and close relationship with him were able to validate him and raise him up in his community.

During our subsequent visits, Felix met us each and every time. The foot I operated on still looked better than his right side, even six years later, when we did our most recent follow-up visit. More touching to me was that every year we met on that dirt and grass runway, the smile on his face couldn't have been brighter. We reconnected, ate together, and shared the warmth of our friendship, not just as doctor and patient but as fellow humans. I would give him my shoes, clothes, beef jerky, peanut butter, or whatever else we had before we departed each time. The language barrier didn't allow for much communication; we spoke mostly in smiles and hugs, but I always felt a tremendous humility and appreciation for the relationship that developed over the years.

The volume of the cases we saw and the amount of teaching we performed increased each year and we were starting to see results. In the time between visits, we continued to raise funds and spread the word of the work we were doing. We visited the Madagascar embassy in the United Nations building in New York and gave lectures to the Shriners, Rotary, and our local branch campus of Penn State University in Altoona. In two separate years we brought Dr. Adrien and one of his colleagues to the States to attend national conferences by the International Pediatric Orthopedic Society.

On our final trip, we teamed up with two rock star physicians from Karolinska University in Stockholm Sweden. Eva Pontièn, MD, and Sahar Nejat, MD, effectively put me out of a job as they enthusiastically stepped up with education and training. My position in the group changed and I was given the call sign The Spider from Sahar. She felt I earned that name because I was able to build the web necessary to connect this fantastic group of individuals. I was very pleased with this promotion. Over the six years of our project, we traveled to and were involved in the education and training of a total of eight different sites across the county.

On several occasions, we visited a Sisters of Charity orphanage in the capital in addition to Heather's orphanage. It housed several hundred children of all ages on a full-time basis, and also hosted various day programs for several hundred more from the local community. We saw young attendants seated at a table, sometimes feeding ten to twelve children simultaneously. I always carried my oversized Nikon camera with me everywhere we went. I had tried to educate my team to keep a low profile so as not to attract attention, but they soon realized and teased me endlessly about this camera, which clearly put a target on our backs. This was certainly an unwanted symbol of American wealth that we really didn't need. I just didn't want to miss an opportunity to document everything we experienced and felt it was worth the risk.

During one of our tours of the orphanage, we found ourselves surrounded by a sea of children, between four and eight years old, all trying to get close to us. I took out my camera and started taking photos of their beautiful faces. After each photo, I turned the camera so that the children could see themselves in the photos. It was probably the first time many of them had ever seen such a large camera or their image in a photo. Each time I showed them a photo, screams of joy rose above the crowd as more children hurried over to be a part of the next one. This continued for several shots, until I had a sudden rush of emotion and my eyeballs began to sweat. I managed to capture two or three more shots before it was all too overwhelming and I had to turn and chase the kids away or I was going to be a blubbering fool in front everyone. It was unbelievable that something as simple as a digital photograph made these children so happy. The sound of their voices screaming and laughing pierced my soul with such deadly efficiency. This was *not* a glancing blow.

Seeing that scene in the orphanage gave me a firm comprehension that my experience paled in comparison to what it is like for millions of others during those often years between birth and meeting an adopted family, or not. It was a scene of survival and compassion for all involved. The attendants were trying to survive emotionally each day, despite being surrounded by so many unfortunate stories. The children were trying to survive from meal to meal, day to day, probably hoping that someday someone would come by and bring them into their own family, where they wouldn't have to fight so hard for any amount of attention.

I felt a special bond and connection with these children. I knew deep down each one was confused, lost, sad, and lonely. From newborns to teenagers, the feeling was the same: Who am I, where do I belong, and what can I do to get an edge up on some of these other equally cute and needy children? I worried about what was going to happen to them. I wanted to tell them all that I had been an orphan as well. I wanted them to know that I turned out okay so they could have hope. I also knew that, given their circumstances, they didn't have the same chances that I had. Walking through the facility and seeing how they lived—the row of ten potties just sitting out in the open, the cribs, the picnic tables they ate at—just seemed so sad and institutional.

I was constantly going back and forth between what I was seeing and trying to imagine what it was like for me. I knew that I had been saved from this, and that most of these kids were not likely to be recycled or find *good families*. Some had a chance, but others did not because of their physical or mental impairments. Probably none of them were likely to experience the warmth and love I had been given in my seat as prince at the Rocco family table. There were times when Kari-Ann and I thought about adopting one of these children. For many reasons, it's nearly impossible for US citizens to adopt a child from Madagascar. In fact, only two children have been adopted by US citizens from Madagascar since 2011. Madagascar is a signatory nation to the Hague Convention on Protection of Children, and with all the legal acrobatics required, the process is extremely difficult. The overwhelming experience of being right in the middle of the country with these children did make the thought cross our minds on multiple occasions.

One child we met at the Sisters of Charity Orphanage was placed there after she was so violently sexually assaulted at the age of twelve that her hip was dislocated in the process. With that injury and stigma, her mother could no longer care for her, and she was brought to the orphanage. Seeing a sixty-year-old nun dressed like Mother Teresa carry this young girl in to see me and ask for my help with her hip was, once again, simultaneously painful and spiritual. I kept staring into the nun's eyes and listening to her plea, which was given with such confidence in my skills even though she didn't know me. Just like with Ed and the wrestling team, she believed in me so much more than I could ever have believed in myself.

I didn't want to let her down and couldn't say no. We attempted to relocate the girl's hip with an open surgery and put her in a body cast. Unfortunately, we had to leave before she healed, but one of the only two orthopedic surgeons in the entire country agreed to follow up with her in our absence. She was lost to follow-up in the system. On a subsequent trip two years later, we couldn't find her anywhere. We had heard that the hip had re-dislocated but no one seemed to have any definite details. I questioned my decision-making in operating on her but tried to remind myself that people *can* walk—sometimes surprisingly well—despite having a hip dislocation.

Four years after that surgery, during our final trip, we were touring the orphanage once again with a completely new OSS team. I was the only one in the group who knew that assault victim's story. I wasn't expecting to see her when we walked into the orphanage—then I spotted her from afar. Our eyes locked onto each other, with electrified air between us as my brain fell silent and I slowly walked toward her. It was as if everyone else in the world had vanished. I said her name and asked how she was. She nodded and smiled. I smiled back and patted her on the shoulder. We had one of those moments where nonverbal gestures were so powerful. We stared at each other for a few more minutes and then said our goodbyes.

I watched her walk away—fairly well, despite the hip disloca-tion—and I realized she was now an attendant herself, taking care of a number of the other children in the long line of succession. I was so grateful and relieved that she seemed happy to see me. I was especially pleased to find that she had fallen onto the right side of the wall, as it would have been so easy for her to have been led astray or downright dragged to the wrong side. Taking care of others seemed to be helping her take care of herself.

Once again, I walked back to the group with quivering lips, a massive lump in my throat and tears in my eyes. I could think of nothing else for several more minutes. Even now, my eyes well up with tears remembering that moment. It was unbelievable to me that I was a part of all of this. It should never have happened in ten thousand years, but it did, and I couldn't have been more fortunate as I did not deserve any of these blessings.

Madagascar was just like Japan. Despite my apprehensions and uncertainty in coming, my willingness to be open to strange and unusual circumstances with a pure heart seemed to bring good things to others and me, as if by magic. Being a chameleon did seem to be my superpower, even though I knew it was also my kryptonite.

With everything we had going on, organizing the visits to Madagascar was becoming another full-time job on top of my regular, already busy career. We continued to sponsor our annual Rocctoberfest celebration, which had now moved out of our back-yard and into the Jaffa Shrine building in order to accommodate the more than seven hundred attendees we had each year. In addition, we were sponsoring an annual OSS Coach purse bingo event, which was starting to raise more money for the mission than the Rocctoberfest event.

Despite all the help, the pressure on my family, and particularly my marriage, wasn't something I was good at balancing. Kari-Ann took on a great deal of the burden of keeping the organization above water. She was part of the team on three of the four trips we took to Madagascar. We were petrified to go, but would leave the children behind with my mother and update our wills before we departed.

Kari-Ann, along with Sandy Pritts, Deb Muri, and too many others to mention, gave more of themselves to OSS than should have ever been asked. As is often (and unfortunately) the case when running a complicated organization with many moving parts, we had a hard time communicating well. Behind the scenes it was becoming a source of much disagreement and division between us. It was all so perfect in so many ways, but it was also becoming way too much for many of us to control.

CHAPTER 8
"HE IS WHO HE IS"

DESPITE MY ATTEMPTS TO DENY IT, I WAS BURNING OUT FAST. Professionally, I was kicking more ass than I should have ever been allowed to kick. Most of my patients loved me and I was one of the busiest surgeons in the practice. I didn't need long to nail down almost anyone's diagnosis. I could often describe my patients' symptoms to them, in a language they could understand, better than they could describe it themselves. That skill seemed to help them feel like I really understood their problem, and I did.

I had heard so many people describe their symptoms so many times that I could almost feel them myself. This wasn't my first rodeo, and I could quickly and inherently sense the patients' concerns consistently, across the board. Blacks, whites, Asians, men, women, it didn't matter. Everyone described the same problem in a very similar manner. Regardless of their occupation or net worth, they all suffered with their difficulty reasonably uniformly. The physical, emotional, or occupational limitations of their problem were fully within my understanding. I could tell them in advance what to expect.

Over the years I seem to have developed a way of talking to my patients that could make almost everyone feel comfortable. I had lived a diverse life and genuinely experienced a broad range of existences. It wasn't contrived. I had a whole repertoire of human understanding to draw from and, as a result, could relate to the blue-collar guys, former military folks, lawyers, old ladies, and young kids alike.

I could also piss someone off or subtly — or not so subtly — get a particular point across to them that they just weren't getting. I couldn't put them through *all* of medical school by way of explanation, but thought I could quickly get to the point of what they needed to take home from their visit. I knew I didn't know everything, but they were seeking *my* opinion, so I usually tried to give it to them whether they were going to like it or not. Most people respected that but some did not. I was there to be honest and as accurate as I could be and knew I could never remember my lies if I started telling them.

After twenty-three years in the profession, and all the changes occurring in medicine, I was wondering if this was really as good as it got. I was approaching my fifties and was sucked into the medical rat race more than I ever wanted. With our increasing trauma coverage at the hospital where I worked and the new electronic medical records system, my practice couldn't have been busier or more complicated to manage. My employer didn't seem to care how good I was or how hard I was working for my patients as long as I continued to comply with the endless e-mails, coding, billing and transcription requirements along with system and government box-checking, and mandatory meetings.

On a typical day, I'd have a full schedule of patients or surgeries and then run out of the office as fast as I could. I was usually trying to make it to whatever sport or performance event our children had that evening. I'd try and stop home to change but if I was running late, I'd find myself standing on the sideline of a soccer match in my shirt and tie. This not only made me feel uncomfortable, but also made me an even bigger target for someone to approach Dr. Rocco for free medical advice.

After the event, the four of us would grab something to eat and then go home, where I would assume my position on the couch to finish the day's charts. This nightly activity was as tedious, mind-numbing, and time-consuming as could be, and I was never caught up. Along with Operation Small Steps and Shriners, which I enjoyed, the arbitrary government-mandated manner in which I had to practice medicine was slowly eroding my very being.

The life Kari-Ann and I had built with our two beautiful children and oversized home was way more than anything I could have ever expected to achieve. Whether I recognized it or not, however, I was still struggling to see clearly through the fog of my adoption story. After meeting Joyce, I frequently found myself trying to reconcile who I was now with who I *should* have been. I could feel the years of lies piling up on my shoulders and, similar to how many adoptees feel, it seemed as though I was pretending most of my life. Difficulties with our marriage were confounding my confusion even further. I couldn't help feeling like a living version of the Talking Heads song "Once in a Lifetime." *This is not my beautiful life,* I thought.

What's more, the endless hours in front of my laptop were wearing me thin. They weren't so much about any benefit to the patient as they were about capturing charges and flimsy data. *Same as it ever was.* With my impossible workload on any given day, it seemed like I had to choose between being a bad doctor, a bad father, a bad husband, or a bad member of the community. Either way, I was never going to complete all of my seemingly important tasks. I constantly felt like some form of bad Jack.

I was driving the vehicle I called my life much too fast, and felt as if it was ready to fly off the road at any moment. I seriously needed to slow down but couldn't. I thought relocating to a warmer climate, where I didn't also have to plow the driveway at 5 am many mornings between December and April, would help. I realized there was no way in hell I could continue burning the candle at both ends like this for another fifteen years until retirement. I decided to look at a more sustainable lifestyle down south. The family was on board.

Something else made me think that moving away might help

me in the fresh start department as well. Unfortunately, and perhaps in rebellion against my overly-controlled daily existence, bad Jack had been secretly at work trying to blow this perfect life up. Over the previous year or so I had been having an extramarital affair. By the time it was discovered, the affair was over, but email and text evidence still lingered, leading to the revelation.

The discovery of my infidelity couldn't have come at a worse time. I was already in negotiations for a new position and had been emotionally checked out of my current job for some time. Despite our many successes as a family, the constant breakneck pace was seriously killing us mentally, physically, and spiritually.

When I took the position in North Carolina, I mistakenly thought Kari-Ann would reconsider and make the move with me. It didn't work out that way. The infidelity, among other things, was too much for all of us. I couldn't blame her. I loved being a dad and enjoyed my time with the kids immensely. Unfortunately, whether it was my schedule or other reasons, I hadn't been able to be present in the marriage for a while either. As a result, and despite some limited counseling, an impassible stalemate occurred and it ended in a split. Kari-Ann couldn't bring herself to come with me, and I couldn't stay in the current unsustainable work environment. We sold the house, she went north with the kids back to Rhode Island, and I went south to the new job in North Carolina. Complete and total devastation. This was the biggest and most humbling failure of my life. *What the fuck was wrong with me*? I couldn't figure any of it out.

Despite feeling as though I understood my profession and my patients so well, I still understood very little about myself. That made it almost impossible for me to express myself effectively in the marriage. Communication was constantly a struggle and was endlessly maddening. I often felt the frustration of a toddler in not being able to speak my thoughts and feelings to Kari-Ann. Add on that I was a stubborn, independent guy since the day I was born and you can imagine some of the fights Kari-Ann and I had. It was like our marriage never really got into a groove. We were both intelligent people, but nonetheless, it seemed like we still couldn't understand each other. I wasn't even sure which me I was representing at any given time. This must have driven Kari-Ann crazy. Even though it had been brewing for years, the separation seemed to happen so fast.

From the outside, finding Joyce and learning about Larry having Black heritage wasn't really a big deal. Opening Pandora's box in my mind, however, and looking back at my life with the eye-opening realization that none of it was my genuine birthright, had me re-assessing everything. It seemed as though I thought my way into everything I did, when a part of me should have been feeling my way into it. My relationship with Kari-Ann was no different. It didn't seem like she was the person I was supposed to be with. As the layers of paint over my true identity were starting to bubble, crack, and peel away and I was honest with myself, I *never* felt like I was where I was supposed to be. The person I found looking back at myself in the mirror wasn't even the guy I was supposed to be. I could never concede that I might need help with all of the emotional issues that swirled around being adopted. Poking at the wasp's nest of my origin ended up being so much more complicated than outrunning a swarm of wasps. This time, it felt like I was the one on the ground with all the wounds.

I was realizing more and more that I really had to try and *find myself* on my own somehow. With all the secrecy of the adoption, it was like trying to find someone in a witness protection program. I had to stop trying to blend in. My now-familiar skill of chameleonization was simply not sustainable in a marriage when it was a 24/7 ordeal. My colors had to keep changing so often, based on where and who I was with at any given moment, I think I was starting to forget which color I needed to be. Or actually was. When I tried to make my way through the fog of figuring out who I was and how I had brought the collapse of my marriage upon myself, I was reminded of another chameleon I met in Madagascar.

During one of our visits to the Sisters of Charity Orphanage in

Madagascar, we met a boy who has come to represent an earlier post-orphaned version of myself. As we walked into one of the large rooms where the children slept, we saw about thirty boys aged two to six standing in their cribs, all wearing matching orange PJs. Upon entry I snapped a few photos of the group before we continued on our tour. Within less than a minute, while moving along, we were suddenly greeted by one of the children. This three- or four-year-old boy quickly jumped into the procession between Kari-Ann and I and just stood there looking up at Kari-Ann with the biggest, brightest, happiest smile you've ever seen. He posed for a few photos and I showed him the shots on the screen. He was tugging at our pants and just being so damn cute. How could Kari-Ann not pick him up? She was in love.

"Oh my God! He is *so* cute. Look at this guy," she exclaimed.

The sister who was giving the tour introduced him: "This is Matthew."

As he lovingly cuddled Kari-Ann with that perma-grin of his, the conversation quickly evolved into, "Can we keep him? Look at him. He's adorable. Sophia and James would love a new brother."

Oh Geez! Here we go, I thought as I reflexively started envisioning him running around our house and land with our two kids. Due to the country's adoption restrictions, thankfully, I didn't have to be the bad guy in this decision. I would have loved to do something like that, but intimately knew a decision like that should not take place at the emotional spur of the moment.

Our tour guide sister went on to tell us about Matthew. His mother was a mess. She had tried the sisters' patience time after time over the years. She was into drugs and prostitution. At various times, she would get her life together and come back to get Matthew. She'd be involved in the day programs and help around the facility for a while but then would fall off the wagon and drop him back off again. This story made us love him even more but, *my god!* This place was just so freaking sad!

When we looked back at the initial few photos I snapped on entering the bedroom, we saw Matthew again in his pre-cute phase. He was standing bolt upright in his crib with a look of absolute determination on his face. His eyes were focused, his brows were downturned, and he looked like a skilled hunter assessing the situation and planning his attack. In retrospect, his behavior was unusual for a child that age; to randomly approach a strange couple so quickly and eagerly. We then realized he had performed this skit many times before. He saw an opportunity with fresh prey, took his shot, and turned on the charm. You can't blame the guy: we weren't unwilling targets. He seemed to sense that and assessed us with uncanny skill. We loved the attention and entertainment ourselves. It's like he read our minds, knew we were the couple in the group, and just had to have us.

The point is, he somehow innately knew what he was doing. This wasn't preconceived or nefarious in intention per se. He was lost and lonely and probably just trying to find someone to love him consistently. He had to use his personality skills to try and get a leg up on the competition. His natural charisma was his weapon, and he was very skilled at using it to try and survive. He was a master chameleon already. Unfortunately, we departed the facility, probably like many others before us, and burst his bubble once again in the process.

I wonder how many times it took before he was permanently dejected and stopped trying his routine. I, on the other hand, was able to continue with my façade as my parents rewarded it and kept rewarding it over the years. That wasn't necessarily a bad thing.

I had to admit to being more than a little familiar with his tactics. I seemed to have utilized them myself more than a few times over the years. It's clearly not a technique unique to orphans, but found across the scale of humanity. Orphaned children may feel a deeper and more urgent necessity to pull out their particular weapon earlier in life. It's only natural, but given the separation from their natural parents, they may never get to the point where they feel comfortable enough to put it away and just be themselves. It may even get to the point where they use it at times when it's not fully necessary. Depending on their individual level of fear, it may become like shadowboxing.

At what age does a relinquished child start to sense their particular weapon and learn how to use it? Is it three? Two? One? Is it established at birth, upon the initial separation from their parent? James remembered nursing with Kari-Ann when he was two, but at what age are those initial patterns of being a people-pleaser established? No one knows, but why not soon after birth and during separation from the mother? That had to have been a period where survival instincts are pushed to the limit in the struggle to breathe in this new cruel world.

Once established, when does this habit end? At age ten? Twenty-five? Fifty? Never? Is the birth separation trauma so extreme that it sets off a wave of compensatory reactions and natural instincts, causing these children to enter survival mode very early? Not being able to cuddle and bond with their mother likely broke that chain and sent that newborn off to figure life out for themselves. Their only true ally, their partner from the womb, was taken from them and they were on their own to learn about all of life's joys and hazards. No one who looked like them and could be fully and unconditionally trusted by them was present in their life, often right from the beginning. How in the world should they be expected to figure this out on their own? Let's not forget, we give puppies at least six to eight weeks before we take them from their mothers.

Does this happen at the genetic level or strictly in the brain as a part of learning? Are there various gene modifiers or histones employed that alter the shape of the chromosomes to bring out sleeper characteristics necessary for the given situation? Histones are well known to affect DNA to expose or activate various genes during unusual periods to allow the chromosome to ramp up whatever protein or chemical is needed at the time. It is not efficient for us to make every protein we are capable of making when we don't need them. We don't make lactase, the enzyme that digests lactose, until the instant we are exposed to lactose, for instance. The presence of lactose indirectly creates the enzyme necessary for its own destruction. Does maternal abandonment or other stresses create the features necessary to defeat this extreme condition? Do histones affect the DNA of relinquished children in order to provide them with an intense hyperawareness of their situation so they can find a way, any way, to survive? Does this initiate the cascade of fight/flight necessary for survival immediately after birth? Through epigenetics are these changes passed on to that individual's offspring? Geneticists don't fully know, but we do know that our genetic code is able to quickly adapt to any number of varied and extreme conditions present on this planet. We can't always wait for evolution to take place. We often have to adjust quicker than that. It is as if the voice in the adoptee's chromosomes can be heard saying, "Now entering *no mother mode.*"

A side effect of finding Joyce was that the cracks in my worldview of who thought I was were widening. Just like Matthew, it seemed like the majority of my life was spent trying to get people to like me by making them happy. I never wanted to disappoint people and it seemed to have become a habit. Discovering my own sense of nature and biologic connection to actual people seemed to help give me permission to be human, to be consciously selfish. In always seeking to belong, I wasn't necessarily fulfilling my own natural needs and desires to truly just be happy. I just seemed to have slowly found myself so deep in serving everyone else that I couldn't get out. Who was the real me and what did he need? How do I selfishly and tactfully get what I need without hurting someone else? Saying no was never my strong point.

If anything, finding Joyce felt as though I was disappointing her as well in that I didn't, or rather couldn't, fully open my arms and accept her into my life as my mother. I did feel a connection to her, but I already had a mother and she was absolutely perfect. I felt as if I would crush my mother if I told her I had found Joyce. I did also seem to have some connection with this mysterious guy named Larry, or at least with his still unknown racial heritage. My view of who I was, where I was supposed to be, and who I supposed to be with was being questioned even further in my mind.

I had plenty of time to contemplate all of this when I arrived in North Carolina, once again, by myself. For days on end, I sat in my rental apartment and thought. When I got home at the end of a day, I'd sit outside, still in my work shirt and tie, and play video games on my phone. I'd stay there playing and thinking till the sun went down or my battery died. Eating dinner didn't make any sense and I didn't have working cable TV so mostly I just sat and thought. What the hell had gone wrong? We had everything and it still didn't work out. I thought I had done everything I could to create the perfect life which only seemed to have made it all the more imperfect. I loved my job and every step of my career. Medicine was changing and I didn't like many of the changes, but that didn't account for it all.

I wasn't ever truly happy with myself or where I was at any given time. I had talked myself into believing that everything was so ideal and that I should have been happy, but really, I wasn't. It felt as if, my whole life, I was always standing on a foundation of sand below the water. My feet would seek stability and I would gain a foothold from time to time, only for it to be too difficult to maintain as the sand slowly oozed from below me. Finding Joyce helped a little, but being unable to tell my parents about her made it all just seem wrong. She was the other *other woman*, and at various points over the past several years I had been simultaneously cheating on both my mother and my wife. Freaking embarrassing.

I still had very little idea of who I was and what my inner soul needed to be fulfilled. What even was my inner soul? Was that all just a bunch of hippie-dippie baloney or was it something real that could actually be achieved? In Altoona, I was exercising too little, staying up too late completing my charts, and often finishing off the night with too many glasses of bourbon that were tearing apart my gut. Something definitely had to change, but did *everything* have to change? No wife, no kids, no friends, really? Before meeting Joyce, I spent so much time during my life being nurtured, I never really thought much about my nature. Who knows, maybe I did need to spend some time with Jack to see if I could get to know him better.

I thought I knew myself by then but, again, how could I? I had started on this side of a steel door that gave me no connection to my past. Am I not really a continuation of the past and didn't I technically begin before I came into being? Didn't my kids begin with Kari-Ann and I, years before we met, and not on the day they were born? James has my eyelashes and Sophia my yawn. When did those traits begin? Certainly not on the day they were born. They began with me and my father and his mother, dating back forever. How far do those traits go back and whom do they belong to in the first place? In order to truly emerge like the butterfly I was supposed to be, didn't I need to be a caterpillar first? I had to get to know myself better. The adoption and mixed-race identity were really haunting me, and I started wondering more about Larry. I needed to know more about him.

The first step to finding Larry's side of the family started our first Thanksgiving after the separation. I drove up to Rhode Island and then, as a family, we all drove to Erie for the weekend. Joyce lived midway between Erie and Rhode Island and I felt we should stop and say hi on our way back. I also thought that this would be the perfect moment to reveal Joyce's true identity to my children. They were twelve and nine now and I felt they were old enough to understand. Most importantly, being away from them I felt it was important to bring them into the loop of knowing who their father was.

I told the kids in the car, "On the way back, we're going to stop and see the ocelot."

"The what?" they cried in unison.

"The ocelot," I repeated.

"Daddy! What's that supposed to mean?" James asked.

"We're going to meet his real mother," Sophia softly whispered. She nailed it!

The ocelot reference comes from a children's cartoon called *Phineas and Ferb*. In the show, the evil scientist villain, Dr. Heinz Doofenshmirtz, was abandoned by his parents and raised by a pack of ocelots. This accounted for Doofenshmirtz's quirky and pathologic personality traits. I called Joyce the ocelot on that car ride because James once remarked, "Hey, Daddy! Since you don't know your parents, maybe *you* were raised by ocelots?"

"James! What? I was raised by Grama and Papa," I reminded him.

"Oh, yeah, but maybe your real parents were ocelots."

James really did have this whole adoption thing figured out. Why not? Just like in the children's book *Are You My Mother?* by P.D. Eastman, in the world according to James, my mother was just as likely to have been an ocelot as a bird, a tractor, or anything else for that matter.

On the trip to meet the ocelot, we talked about how Joyce and I had reunited, when we met, and why I didn't feel I could tell them at that point. They understood. I told them they couldn't tell Grama and Papa just yet and they understood. It was a completely genuine moment and it felt great to get all of this off my chest. I spoke to my children about my adoption for the first time with absolutely honest, adult intentions, and they got it. They were more prepared and able to accept it than I gave them credit for.

As we arrived in Mansfield, we walked into her museum and everyone was excited, Joyce most of all. She had hinted to me and slipped into conversations more than a few times that she wanted the kids to know her as their grandmother. She knew I didn't want to do that to my mother but that didn't stop her from suggesting it would be a good idea. Looking back, since the day we met, she'd done everything other than outright tell me some form of that request. I had kept her from enjoying that and now could sense she completely appreciated it finally coming to fruition.

The kids were great with it and everything fit nicely into place for them. They now understood why Joyce did all those grand-motherly things like talk *just to them* and knit them hats and

Christmas stockings for the fireplace. They totally understood and didn't have any hard feelings for not knowing earlier. Sophia said, "It's your life, Daddy. We didn't have to know everything."

We had a great conversation about it during our drive afterward and I was impressed with the depth of our discussion on adoption and unwanted pregnancies. I mentioned to them why it might hurt my parents' feelings to find out about Joyce. I explained that Grama and Papa raised me and I was every bit their child as well. I worried they would feel hurt if they thought they were losing me to a mother who hadn't raised me. The kids knew not to tell my parents, but I sensed I couldn't trust James for long. Like his father, he was burdened with not having much of a filter between his brain and his mouth. I felt this was a great first step in coming clean with my parents. Having my children meet Joyce as their birth grandmother went so well that I decided I needed to find my father's side of the family first.

Through Joyce's research, she had found that Larry had died the year before I met her. At the time, it really didn't register in my brain as a loss. As an adoptee, when you're going through this process it is impossible to grasp all the interconnected and often subconscious feelings of loss, mourning, regret, and downright confusion. You don't know what you don't know. I was starting to sense that it was very important for me to know him as best as I could.

Joyce was able to help by using her genealogy skills to quickly locate one of Larry's brother's obituaries. We struck the jackpot in that we found I had a cousin, Jay, living in Fayetteville, North Carolina, only about ninety minutes from me. I tried to call him a few times but he never picked up. I felt weird leaving a message saying, "Hi, I am your Uncle Larry's missing bastard son." I found his address and decided to take a drive to his house to leave a letter at his door. He wasn't home, but I called his number again and this time left a message explaining the letter and who I was. He replied within an hour and agreed to meet.

I met Jay in his car, parked outside of a Men's Warehouse

clothing store, after he had just gotten out of church. Not knowing what to expect, I was excited but somewhat hesitant to meet him. I was so focused on the nuts and bolts of making that initial contact, I had no idea what to say or what to expect when I met him. Still, I was calm and even businesslike. I had been through it with Joyce once already. With everything that happened over the years I was accustomed to never knowing where things would bring me, but was generally optimistic. Jay, however, was completely blindsided.

I parked my car down a few spaces so I wasn't immediately next to him. I walked up to the driver's window and said, "Jay?"

"Yeah, get in," he replied.

Jay is a big guy, probably six foot, large-framed with a medium brown complexion. He was sharply dressed in a purple suit with an expensive-looking watch and a few gold rings on his fingers. It was his Sunday suit for attending a Baptist service at church. I felt like a total nerd in my basic white-boy jeans, polo shirt and light shell jacket as I walked over, opened the door, and sat in the passenger seat.

Right from the start, he was polite and stoic and I'm sure experiencing a good deal of confusion over how he got dragged into this whole mess.

"Sorry for interrupting your Sunday with this," I apologized.

"It's okay. What's up?" I could immediately tell from the start that he wasn't going to give me any clues as to what he was thinking.

"Well, I was adopted and about eleven years ago I found my mother," I started. "She told me your uncle Larry was my dad."

I grabbed my phone and quickly pulled up the photo I'd had saved in my favorites folder for some time. It was a black-and-white photo of Larry from his senior year that I showed to people when they asked to see him. With that information and this photo, the resemblance left little doubt that we were related.

"I know Larry passed away in 2006, but I recently decided to try and find his side of the family," I explained, trying to slowly and confidently match his demeanor. "I got your name out of an obituary from when your father passed. I saw that you lived only an hour and a half from me so I gave it a shot. I don't really know what I'm looking for but just thought I'd try to make contact."

"Okay, that's cool," he replied. "I don't honestly know much about Larry. You see, there were eight brothers in the family and, you know, they didn't all get along so well. So it's been a long time since I've seen him. I have some photos at home we could try and copy if you want. I'll ask around but I don't really have much to tell you."

"Okay, that'll work," I told him.

"Cool, follow me."

I got out of his car, got into mine, and started following him to his house. It was that fast. Within ten minutes of meeting we were driving in separate cars back to his house. He later told me that on the ride there, he called his mother and said, "Ma, this guy showed up today and says he's Larry's son. Ma, this guy's legit. He walks like us, he has pigeon toes like us, he's a little sassy like us, and his pants don't fit him on the back because his butt sticks out like us." Really? What the hell? Why was he even looking?

Apparently after Jay told her that, his mother told him, "Jay, he is who he is. Answer his questions as best you can."

When Jay told me what his mother said, my jaw dropped. I am who I am? *I* am who I am? I *AM* who I am! It was so simple and yet I never thought of it that way. It had been fifty-one years and I had never once considered that was an option. Really? His state-ment struck me dumb and I paused in mid conversation on the phone while he continued talking and just stared. Wow! Like a thorn being pulled from my paw, that just made all the difference.

Even though I didn't necessarily know who I was, I always was who I was. I knew I was adopted and should have known that meant I had birth parents that were real people. It sounds really ridiculous, but adopted children don't always have that option to know they came from real people. These mystery parents develop sometimes multiple imaginary personas on their own based on who the adoptee wants them to be. The parents may be looked at as good or evil, rich or poor, loving or mean. It didn't matter who I wanted them to be; I had now found a connection to both of them and had my foundation. I had my stability. That simple bit of information was key and came with a firm calming sense that I could now begin to put the pieces of myself together more accurately—with real people who were once a couple, even if only briefly, as a foundation. I didn't have to imagine or guess anymore.

Then a wave of terror rushed over me. What role did my parents and family play in who I was? Was I losing a part of me that I loved and wasn't ready to discard? I couldn't negate their role and the influence they had on me. It didn't take long before I thought, *A lot! They still had a whole lot to do with who I was.* A good part of my existence was their nurturing, their stories, their morals, their quirkiness. I was just as much a part of my parents and my family as I was Joyce and Larry. Knowing Joyce and Larry did seem to give me a necessary sense of stability, of my nature. There it is! There is the answer. For years I had been dominated by my nurturing and that gave me success within society but I never seemed to be happy with myself. That's what was missing: an understanding of and an acceptance of my nature. Both my nature and my nurture were affecting my daily life, but I didn't know which was the nature part.

Maybe that's what separates adopted kids from *real kids*. To me, real kids always seemed to have more confidence in themselves. Good or bad didn't matter. Whatever they were they seemed authentic. Real kids have grown up seeing their nature in their parents, and their nurturing was often in line with their parents' nature. It was all they knew. They didn't question their existence and there was no cognitive dissonance between their nature and nurture. I didn't feel authentic and this seemed to sometimes cause conflict for me. My nurturing was fantastic, but there was often an underlying conflict with my nature in that I didn't necessarily see myself in my family's personalities or appearance. It was no one's fault, it just was. I didn't ever even recognize it as a thing, but it was a thing. I just went along and tried to be like them, even if it didn't feel natural or authentic.

On occasions when I saw or felt my nature and it conflicted with my nurture, I thought it was a demon. Being Catholic didn't help either. I worked too hard studying, was too smart, and didn't feel like I fit in, so I felt guilty for getting good grades. I often downplayed my academic success and couldn't really enjoy it, but I did enjoy helping others on the tests. I was too dedicated to my work and not spending enough time with the family, so I felt guilty. I enjoyed being social and having too much fun with my friends when maybe I should have been studying or with my family, so I felt guilty. I felt guilty whether I was being good Jack or bad Jack because I didn't know which one I was supposed to be. It seemed like I could only be one, but the two seemed to be in a constant battle. The other problem is that I never really looked at either as purely bad or good. My parts weren't necessarily good or bad, just different from my surroundings.

My nature was a little bit of both my birth parents. Maybe I worked hard and studied hard because of Joyce and her academic curiosity. Maybe I was a little bit of a social butterfly because of Larry. I didn't feel bad when I was studying or partying, but I felt guilty for doing either because I was raised in a family that hadn't experienced higher education or socializing the way I had. They were all about the family and togetherness and I appreciated that as well. I just had other facets in addition. Me going away to college and becoming president of the fraternity felt like I was leaving the family circle that I loved. Neither me nor my family wanted that, but my nature may have been pulling me and I couldn't resist. My family provided me with a safe environment in which to exercise my freedom, but it seemed I couldn't necessarily be fully myself in that environment either, so I was always wandering.

While we were at his house, Jay brought out a photo of Larry with his seven brothers from their mother's funeral. It was the last time they were all together. We drove around and talked while we went to a few pharmacies to find one where we could copy the photograph. He said his mother was calling around to see what everyone else knew.

Larry's story wasn't as neat, clean, and easily understandable for me as Joyce's. From a photograph I saw of her parents, I could tell that Larry's mother was mixed-race. Her father was a dark-skinned Black man and her mother was as white as could be. Current DNA tests have revealed these divisions of race to be much more complicated and often less relevant than was believed in the past, but in general, that meant Larry was closer to 60 to 75 percent African American, not the 12 percent we initially suspected. His brothers ran the gamut of shades from dark to very light. One of the brothers was a Black Panther in the sixties. Some of the brothers were apparently light-skinned enough that they lived their lives as white. For at least one brother, his wife wasn't aware of his race until his funeral, when the Black side of the family showed up. Larry was somewhere in the middle. The eight brothers apparently had a number of personal issues and not all of them kept in touch with each other. We copied the photo, exchanged phone numbers, and said our goodbyes.

On my way home, Jay called me and left a voice message. This previously suspicious and stoic man was now excited like a teenager. "Jack! Hey, man, call me back," he said. "I found out some things. Call me back as soon as you can. This is important."

I returned the call and he told me, "Hey, man, I talked to my aunt. Turns out you have four half siblings and they're all living in North Carolina."

I had been living in North Carolina for about six months and had decided to start looking for my family about three weeks before. It took me less than a month to find a cousin and four half siblings all living within three hours of me. It was like living in a Hallmark movie, but once again I could not get my brain to accept that it was real.

Later that night after meeting Jay, before I could connect with my siblings, I spoke to my new aunt Claudia. She filled me in on

Larry. She mentioned that Larry was an alcoholic and had issues with his racial identity. "Larry was too white for the Blacks and too Black for the whites," she told me. Larry's oldest son with his wife, who was white, was only five months younger than me. Seems as though papa was a rolling stone.

I later learned that my siblings' mother had put another child up for adoption when she was sixteen. Getting pregnant for the second time, she couldn't bring herself to relinquish another child. She decided to keep the child, and Larry's father encouraged him to do the right thing and marry her. They were married and had two more boys and a girl. At some point, Larry left the family, and later died while working in New Jersey as a limo driver. Claudia wasn't sure how he died, but "it was probably from drinking," she told me.

This, of course, upset me quite a bit. Over the next month or so, I met two other cousins, Richelle and Necole, and Larry's only surviving brother, Gene.

Meeting and spending time with Gene was incredibly powerful for me. His daughter Necole was fantastic in holding the reunion in her beautiful home outside of Richmond. Richelle came down from Maryland as well for the event. I seemed to naturally fall into the rhythm and demeanor of the group. We had spoken a few times on the phone prior. Meeting Gene and feeling his calming presence gave me a palpable feeling of comfort. He was so cool. "Damn, you are the spittin' image."

From Gene I learned that Larry was something of a softy. "Larry was sensitive," he told me. "One time I came home and Larry was back from college. My mother told me he was down at the lake fishing. When I got down there, Larry was teaching some retarded kid how to fish. Larry liked retarded kids."

Larry's degree was in special education and he worked as a teacher for years. Gene told me that Larry was turned down for a promotion that he felt he was most qualified for "because he was Black." He eventually left education, left the family, and started driving a limo in Atlantic City.

On the football field, Gene said, "Larry was a bull." He explained to me that Larry was the guy they always gave the ball to when they needed extra yards in a clutch: "He could run through anyone."

Gene proudly shared that he played football as well. Gene was scheduled to begin training camp for the Minnesota Vikings but was drafted into the Vietnam War before he could start. When he came back from the war, he played in the Canadian Football league for a while until he broke his ankle. I guess football ran in the family, and that somewhat explained my affinity for the game and my speed during high school.

I eventually met all of the siblings — first my sister and youngest brother, along with their mother, and then the other two brothers at a potluck dinner they invited me to. We have continued to stay in contact, they were very polite but initially obviously quite shocked and dumbfounded. They'd had no knowledge of my existence and, given the circumstances, were understandably suspicious and wrapped in their own emotions.

During this potluck dinner, they showed me photos of Larry and gave me a larger sense of who he was. It wasn't all rosy from their standpoint either. Larry left the family when they were fairly young and they mentioned that he was sometimes referred to as a "deadbeat dad." I didn't dig too much into their relationship but got the sense that they weren't his biggest fans. Once again, it didn't seem as though it was any of my business, and my brain still couldn't grasp the fact that Larry was my *real* father either.

At our first meeting, my new brother Christopher's initial reaction to me was epic. He has a very outgoing personality and has spent most of his life at the North Carolina shore running a tackle store and chartering fishing trips. He walked into the backyard and was working the crowd like a politician.

"Hey Joe, Topher! How are y'all? You're both getting so big," he said, greeting my new nephews while approaching the area where I was standing.

Then he walked closer, looked me in the face, and quickly

turned his eyes away. "Whoa!" he exclaimed, and diverted from the path he had been walking, as if trying to get away from me. "You must be Jack." He recovered and came over to shake my hand. "I'm Chris." After doing so, he turned away again as he reiterated his reaction. "Man, I'm wiggin'."

Apparently, my physical appearance and similarity to our father was freaking him out a little bit. Turns out, I look more like Larry than any of them. I wasn't sure if I was fully welcome at that point or not. I got a sense that they were all being nice in inviting me but somewhere deep in their buried, partially traumatized childhood, they weren't totally excited to be seeing him/me again. I worried that they might be thinking, "Oh no! Not him again. I thought we got rid of him when he died."

It bothered me that Larry had left his family, especially since I was currently going through a separation myself. I felt absolutely horrible that I wasn't with my kids. I love my children more than anything and never wanted to harm them in any way. I loved my wife as well but the flood of memories as I relived my past couldn't compute that I was destined to be with her. I heard the stories and saw how much Larry's departure affected his wife and children, and I was ashamed that I appeared to be doing the same thing. The realization that I seemed to be following in my father's footsteps was hanging heavy on me. I felt as if I was the son of Frankenstein in unknowingly becoming like my biological father without ever having met him. Although my family was always welcome to join me in North Carolina, given the circumstances and my own stupidity, the end result did seem similar to him leaving the family for New Jersey.

Of course, no two situations are ever the same but we did seem to be experiencing some similarities. I wanted to understand Larry and put him in a good light. I wanted to forgive him, and in turn, myself, for the similarities in our struggles with marriage. I wanted to believe that he loved his children but perhaps was rushed into a marriage that he wasn't quite ready for. Maybe he wasn't self-aware enough or too busy and could never reconcile that with any difficulties he may have been having with his wife and his internal struggle with being mixed-race. It was highly complicated and too much to be thinking about during my first reunion with my siblings. How much of it was really my business, anyway? I really didn't know and didn't want to pry, but the similarity in our situations didn't go unnoticed. I wanted to give both him and myself the benefit of the doubt.

I was also curious about the comment that he was "too white for the Blacks and too Black for the whites." That concept shocked me and gave me the same sense of what I felt as the Italian blue-collar kid. I felt too low class for the upper class and too upper class for the low class. Does it work in both positive and negative ways? Was I making it all up as I went along, trying to backfill the life I was deconstructing in retrospect? I had no idea.

The thought kept running through my head: "How in the hell am I turning out just like Larry when I never met him?" I was just like Joyce without having met her. I was also just like my parents and Italian family. Finding out small bits of information about my birth parents made me feel as though I was finally standing on three very solid pillars of bedrock, despite a lifetime as an adoptee constantly feeling insecure. I realized, for the first time, that the sense of the ground shifting below my feet had stopped. It was a palpable sensation of calm and a more concrete understanding of myself. Finally, at fifty-one, despite my newfound flaws, I was beginning to sense, understand, and accept that I indeed was who I was.

Now how would I tell everyone?

PART THREE
FREE WILL

"That's the thing about free will: Every decision we make is a choice against something as much as it is for something else."

REBECCA SERLE, WHEN YOU WERE MINE

CHAPTER 9
HIS STORY CHANGES EVERYTHING

"HISTORY IS A COLLECTION OF LIES THAT EVERYONE AGREES UPON," Napoleon once said. "History is written by the victors" is a well-quoted line from Churchill. Taken together, the quotes seem to imply that as long as you win, you can write all the lies you like. Clearly this is not how it is intended. With privilege should also come responsibility for the accuracy of history, as there are valuable lessons on both sides of the battle. What exactly does accurate history mean? Whose point of view is most accurate? It's not as straightforward as it would initially seem.

Humans are intimately tied to their stories and their lies, and sometimes it's difficult to differentiate between the two. Our ability to tell stories and make up oral and written accounts of our existence seems to be one of the single greatest characteristics leading to the evolutionary success of civilized man. Our stories, and our culture in general, both overtly and covertly tie our existence to our concepts of morality, good versus evil, and success versus failure. Was Columbus a great Italian explorer who discovered the New World or someone whose actions initiated the devastation of the Incas, Mayans, and countless other indigenous cultures? Was Columbus really to blame or was he just the guy who happened to be there at the time? I guess it depends on your history and perspective.

Very few cultures tell stories where they come across as the bad guys. Many individuals have fought and died defending that honor of goodness for their God, country, and family. These stories are also a fundamental way in which we learn about who we are, and who belongs with us. It also implies who is safe and what might harm you.

From what I'd been learning, the origins of my life were simultaneously tied to both the boarding of the Mayflower in England and to slave ships leaving Africa for America. Those two events may very well have also happened around the same general time period (1619-1620). The story, which I lived with all these years, however, involved emigrating on a totally different ship from Italy. The melding of those three simultaneous and incongruous stories was a little inconceivable and difficult to absorb. Which story was truly mine—or were they all equally mine? This was clearly not typical, but was exactly what I was working with.

I believe, ignorance is truly the one of the greatest sins of all. Not in that you don't know but in that you know but choose to *ignore* the truth. How could I ignore all that? It really became very disrupting to my general thoughts on my identity as I had come to understand it.

What the hell *was* my story?

I had so many ideas going through my head with my new perspective that it was hard for me to keep things straight. Before I could explain everything to others, I needed to tell my parents. It was all so confusing, but I had to get it all right in my heart and mind. I found myself trying to work it out by practicing on my nearest and dearest friends. There were only so many people I could trust.

Soon after finding Larry's side of the family, I took a trip back to Altoona. I met up with Stephen Pyo, the PA I worked with for most of the thirteen years I spent in practice there. Stephen is probably a bigger package of drama, hype, and adrenaline than I could ever be. He would say the opposite. During our time together, we fought valiantly against many a worthy opponent, whether that be nurse, hospital administrator, or noncompliant patient. When we battled together, we felt it was beautiful, effective, and that we got our points across with passion and finality. Unfortunately, when we went toe-to-toe with one another, it could get ugly, like drunken brothers throwing beer cans at each other in the parking lot of a family reunion. We were both too much alike to not get into these occasional scuffles, but we never carried a grudge or had long-term bad feelings over our disagreements. He was part Italian as well.

Over a beer, I told Stephen about my discoveries. The last he'd heard of the story, I had met Joyce and knew that my father was part Black and possibly part Italian or middle Eastern. Stephen spent years in the operating room listening to my stories of growing up in Erie, hanging out with all my Italian cousins and aunts, eating pasta after church, surviving my Philadelphia residency, and traveling across the globe to Japan. I was like Alyson Hannigan's character in *American Pie* starting every story with "This one time, at band camp…" Only my stories started "This one time, in Japan…" We did a lot of surgeries together and I like to talk during surgery, so he'd heard all these tales repeatedly. He can probably tell them better than I can.

After I told him about meeting Jay and my half siblings, he went back to asking about Joyce and her heritage. Then he paused, and I could tell he was confused.

"So where does your Italian side come from?" he asked.

"Well, genetically, there's none," I told him.

"Dude! That is so fucked up. All these years that's all you talked about, was being Italian," he reminded me.

"I know, but it wasn't true," I apologized.

"That's fucked up because you look Italian. You are still Italian, right?" he begged for confirmation.

"I don't know. I think so but not really, I guess. I don't know," I stammered. "You've met my dad, he's like 200 percent Italian, right? The nuns were smart back then. I guess they figured out to put the mulatto kids with the Italians and no one would know. I don't feel totally English or African either but I guess I am, sort of. I need a ruling on this one."

"You're still Italian," he reassured me with confidence.

The thing that made me Italian in his eyes was my story. That's what I hung onto all these years as well. I used that story my whole life as a base upon which to explain myself to others. Over the past few years, my story had changed so frequently and dramatically that I was getting confused. I couldn't just ignore this new information and pretend it didn't exist, but I was having a difficult time stitching it all together in my mind. I couldn't deny that I had many features, characteristics, and traits of my birth parents. My story had taken a dramatic twist over the past several years and it was strangely upsetting to the view I had developed of my surroundings and myself. Trying to explain who I was kept getting more complicated, but at least it was closer to the truth than it had been. I was recycled and, in many ways, difficult to catalog but, as Jay's mother would say, I was who I was.

Finding Joyce tied me to the Mayflower and the founding of our country. I could envision that side of my family, like an old Western movie I watched with Uncle Joe, pioneering across the land, fighting the redcoats or the Indians as they sat around trying to decide which laws they should keep from England and which ones they had to eliminate. I was proud of that because it was a part of that great American story I'd been told my whole life. As an immigrant Italian kid, I always looked at it as *their* story but not really mine. Now it was a part of mine as well.

I was perfectly comfortable with Joyce's story when I learned it. She told me she never wanted children, and didn't want to marry that young, so in the sixties, what else was she supposed to do? It made me think of one of the many ways you can apologize in Japanese. The word *zanen* generally means "I'm sorry, but as you know, that is just the way it is and no one can do anything about it." An Italian might say, "What are you gonna do? Fuggedaboutit." In any language, though, I understood what happened. She didn't have a choice, it's just how things were back then.

I remember telling Kari-Ann that meeting her was the best possible scenario. Over the years, I grew to understand her like I understood my children. When we spoke, I knew where she was coming from. We visited each other a number of times at my house or hers, and she was very open but never imposing. She was very focused on her work but also laid back in the ways of the world. She never pressured me and was always excited when we communicated. She was just how I might be if I were in her shoes.

She probably wanted more from me but also understood the forces that were pulling me away or keeping me from getting too close. She was very concrete about the relationship and not overly emotional. Perfect.

Unfortunately, Larry's side of the story wasn't so neat and clean. Suddenly finding out my origins ran through the era of slavery, cotton fields, lynchings, and segregation brought with it a great deal of cringeworthy thoughts and painful emotions. Living fifty years of my life without this knowledge was especially unsettling. What did it all mean? I had absolutely no idea. More than a few friends mentioned to me that had I known earlier, I might have qualified for special grants or scholarships during school. "Great!" I rolled my eyes in disbelief. That was the least of my concerns at this point. I was still trying to figure out who the hell I was. For me, it was impossible to ignore, and being adopted had progressively gotten a lot more complicated over the years.

As I divulged this information to many of my oldest and dearest friends, many seemed to be able to look back, jump off the fence, and say things such as, "Now that you mention it..." The whole experience forced me travel back in time as well and re-evaluate myself and all the influences in my life with this new perspective. It was an academically interesting endeavor but very much a distraction that never seemed to go away.

When I looked back and recalled my relationships with the Black secretaries, janitors, and women I dated in Philly, it wasn't really uncomfortable for me. When I got along with my buddy Lonnie in Japan, or with the 4x400 relay team, I wasn't faking it. I *was* able to naturally get along with them well, and seemingly better than my white friends. It was the same with my Black patients. I seemed to be able to speak and understand their language on a natural level long before I ever knew I was mixed-race. It wasn't something I necessarily had to be taught. I'm sure a large part of this was because of my blue-collar upbringing. But now I was wondering, was it because I was mixed race, too?

I blended in many places, whether I was in Japan or Pennsylvania. My inherent knowledge of Black cultural mannerisms or sympathy for their struggle seemed to be a part of who I was, not disingenuous. It was becoming more blatantly obvious that it was with me this whole time but was often cleverly disguised under a veil of culture, making it difficult to see for myself and others.

Fortunately, as I went back, I couldn't really recall any major ugly racist statements I'd made or feelings I'd had. I did own the fact that publicly denying my secret love interests was clearly discriminatory, and couldn't deny that guilt. The economic divide between Blacks and whites I witnessed in Philadelphia became more curious to me. As I got to know some of the worst iconic stereotypes of the inner city at the time, I truly liked a good number of these individuals at a personal level. I wasn't naïve and certainly wouldn't trust many of them in a dark alley at night. However, from my position of trust as their physician, I seemed to be able to see through *their* cultural facade of "tough street guy" persona a good deal of the time. In their position of medical vulnerability, I saw the same pain, fear, and uncertainty that I saw in my white, Hispanic, or Asian patients. There was no fundamental difference.

I was waking to the fact, however, that if my *natural self* didn't coincide with my nurtured cultural identity, I often subdued those feelings and went with the crowd. If we're honest with ourselves, we should all recognize that phenomenon. I really didn't think much for myself, or if I did, it was always within the Italian Catholic blue-collar cultural constraints I grew up in. That's what I had been taught, but what I felt sometimes collided with this education. This isn't unique to adoptees, but may be more internally obvious to them, as they already don't always feel like they fully belong and have become accustomed to blending. Some adoptees perhaps recognize that they don't and can't fit in and just say "Fuck it, I'm going to be a rebel." The difference between what the subconscious *feels* and the outer brain *thinks* is where I believe a good deal of the cognitive dissonance that adoptees describe comes from.

If I was too close to Black people, I worried it might look to my colleagues and friends as though I was being overly sympathetic or as if I carried some internal demon within me. I got along with white or Italian people as well and was able to do that in the confines of my society without question. I was never specifically told I couldn't bring a Black woman to the orthopedic dinners; it just seemed as though it would be awkward. It couldn't just be. For some reason if I got along with Blacks as a white person, I had to somehow be able to explain that. As an adoptee, not knowing my history and not being confident in myself, I couldn't explain that—so I went with a white girl. I recognized that I had been doing a lot of explaining throughout my life, even to myself, trying to reconcile those discrepancies between what I thought and what I felt.

After journeying into Larry's life, I had developed two broad and probably equally inaccurate views of him. Deadbeat dad, alcoholic, and playboy—or sensitive special education teacher who was fun, liked "retarded kids," and could run over anyone on the football field. It was very sparse information to be sure. I quickly saw that there was no sense in digging any further into the opinions of others. Joyce could represent herself, but I soon realized that Larry, like everyone else, was far from one-dimensional. I knew I'd either hear downright lies, or the people who knew him would just tell me what they thought I wanted to hear. He was just as complicated as anyone else, and opinions on him were falling all across the spectrum.

I didn't really like Larry's story as it stood. The fact that I was the son of a womanizing, mixed-race, football-playing alcoholic wasn't something I wanted to put on my curriculum vitae. It did ground me somewhat from an intellectual and emotional stand-point, in that I could now more colorfully see who he was and how others viewed him. Even if I didn't like the cultural stereotypes the view gave of him, the opinions did often give more of a view into the person who was doing the explaining than it did to capture Larry's essence. I managed to do fairly well professionally with this sensitive tenacity I received from him, whereas Larry seemed to have fallen onto the other side of the American dream with it. We were definitely not playing on the same field.

Larry graduated from college, so you would think that would have given him more opportunities. It appeared that he did have more opportunities, they just didn't seem to pan out for him. My father never went to college, but was in a close-knit, supportive family structure. Larry lived out the last of his days in a small one-bedroom apartment in Atlantic City driving a limo, whereas my father was surrounded by friends and family no more than a quarter of a mile away from his favorite living room chair. I'm not saying either is better or worse, I'm just looking at differences and deviations from the societal norm. To be fair, maybe I'm describing the white societal norm that I grew up with.

The most glaring difference between my father and Larry was clearly race, but even that was clouded. Larry was Black but really light enough to pass as "light skinned," Middle Eastern, or maybe Italian to those who didn't know. But Larry really seemed to be culturally Black. What gave him his Blackness? I found myself trying to figure out what that even meant for him, and in turn, that part of me.

I rationalized that, despite the infidelity and my marriage falling apart, my story was *different* from Larry's. That my story could be explained *differently*. I wasn't the son of Frankenstein. The emotional aspect of how I was falling in closer step with the apparent villain in the story than the hero really bothered me. I wanted to understand Larry better, but he wasn't around to tell his side of the story.

My father was a product of his time and station in life, just like so many other fathers of his generation. Similarly, Larry was probably a product of his circumstances and generation as well. What was it like to be a mixed-race Vietnam War veteran going back to college in the mid-1960s? What was it like to be mixed at a time when lines were drawn so starkly in the sand between white and Black? That was the only way I could look at Larry accurately. I couldn't compare him directly to a Black or white or mixed-race male of today. I had to look at him under the microscope of the time and place he was raised to be able to fully understand him. In a way I did understand him, because I was better understanding myself and starting to dissect out the Black, white, Italian, male, oldest son, and adoptee parts of me. I had found myself developing into a freaking Rubik's cube over the years, to be sure.

I started looking into Larry's side of the story, trying to find an answer to why he looked like the bad guy. Let's face it; Larry did seem to be a little popular with the ladies. Both Joyce and my siblings' mother seemed to be fond of him and both mentioned that he could be very charming. I think in general the sense was that Larry was fun and they liked hanging out with him. No one claimed that he had committed any crimes or assaulted anyone. He certainly wasn't the only guy in the sixties who got a woman pregnant and didn't marry her. The number of adoptions after World War II, especially of mixed-race children, show this to have been common. That wasn't exclusively a Black guy thing either; white guys did it too. Interracial relationships were just much less likely to result in marriage. The birth control pill wasn't approved by the FDA until 1960, and condoms weren't easily available or accepted either. Birth control was very much a foreign concept in those days and, together with the sexual revolution, clearly had unintended consequences. Was this all Larry's fault? It seems like he, like everyone else, was just living in very difficult and changing times without any accepted road map to follow.

What was Larry's story?

I felt I knew the British side of my story fairly well from all my American history classes. From Papa, I knew the immigrant story intimately as well, but I didn't really understand the Black side of the story. Why was it that Blacks as a stereotypical whole seem to be the exception to the American success rule? There were many stories of greatness, yet the group still seemed to struggle to achieve the same degree of assimilation that other ethnicities seemed to enjoy. This rabbit hole seemed to just get deeper and more complex as I ventured down. I couldn't help but find that every road I traveled down eventually led me through the mass involuntary relocation and slavery of Black people.

What were the stories Larry heard? What would my Black grandfather have told his children and grandchildren? How would that have affected Larry? Just as I learned my Italian heritage from Papa, I had to imagine what my Black grandfather would have taught about living in America. What would Larry have passed along to me about what it was like growing up Black or mixed-race in the 1960s? It didn't take long for me to imagine that Papa and my Black grandfather would have painted quite different stories.

Papa always told me this was the land of opportunity and would say, "You're smart, Jack. You can do whatever you want." What would my Black grandfather have told me about my past and my hopes and dreams for the future in the sixties and seventies? Probably that I was going to have to work harder than anyone else. That I was going to have to fight like hell. I couldn't deny that the difference of those early stories and beliefs alone was likely to have made a significant impact on my view of the world and how I fit into it.

I'm not an expert in African-American history: I had the opportunity to receive these lessons many times, but rejected them. I never had much of an affinity for history as a whole, as it didn't seem relevant to my purpose. I didn't have a "real" past for the longest time and history really had no connection to me or me to it. As an adoptee, I was just trying to survive. Now history had taken on a new meaning. I wasn't merely learning what a bunch of dead people did; it was actually relevant information tied to my alter ego and all those lost family members I never knew. This was in large part about Larry and his story, and I finally wanted to hear about it.

I had to teach myself about my historical past, and felt I had to hear it from Blacks themselves. I started reading and watching documentaries, not as someone interested in acing a test but as a newly anointed Black man—if I can even say that—interested in unraveling the most difficult Gordian knot known to man: himself. Important figures would come up in conversation—Jesse Owens, Ruby Bridges, the Scottsboro Boys—and I'd linger there a bit longer. When I wasn't filling in missing gaps from the history I'd been taught, I was looking at history from a new perspective. I didn't see Rosa Parks as a Black woman sitting on a bus any longer. Now I saw her as a woman sitting on a bus who happened to be Black. Race always seems to be an issue, but can also be cleverly spun or highlighted by the order of the adjectives to place emphasis on the desired focus. Rosa Parks now looked very similar to the photos of Larry's mother and my many new aunts on Larry's side. With that new perspective she immediately became a woman first and Black second. It's surprising how everything changes when the people you learn about look like you or your family.

Similarly, being exposed to such inner-city violence as a young man during residency made me astutely aware of the cultural and economic divide between Blacks and whites, but I really never gave much thought to the origins of the problem.

Looking back, I clearly remember having these conversations with my patients many times over the years in Philly. One patient in particular, who sustained nine gunshot wounds prior to one hospitalization, told me straight out when I asked him.

"Robert, you're a good guy and seem really smart, man. Why is it that you're out there selling crack? The way Philly is set up you can just walk in any direction and in less than a half hour you'd be out of this mess."

"Doc, I ain't got no choice, it's all I know," he said.

Is that true or not? I'm not going to debate the question, but that was the perception of reality for many of the men and women growing up at that time in those neighborhoods.

I found myself thinking deeply about why so many Black men were in prison in the first place. You don't get into prison unless you're a criminal, right? Or does it just mean it's because you were arrested, and those are two very different things? What really makes someone a criminal anyway? By the demographics in the prisons it does seem to more often be color not criminality.

Irish street gangs and crime in New York during the late 1800s weren't uncommon following the wave of Irish immigration to America. Random street shootings during the days of Al Capone and the Chicago mob wars were certainly a blemish on the Italians during Prohibition as well. The Kennedys also rose to wealth and power under the auspices of crime and violence during Prohibition. Without much digging, you can easily find the British founders involved in violent actions against indigenous people and Blacks over the years. That was never looked upon as a crime. Was this any different than the crime scenes I witnessed in inner-city Philadelphia? Act for act it didn't seem to be, but on the other hand, it was fundamentally different in that the Italians, Irish and British seemed to use this anomaly of a crime-filled past as a stepping stone. Assimilation seemed to be happening slower and with more roadblocks for the Blacks.

Now, most Italians were not involved with the Mafia and most Irish were not bootleggers, but each of those ethnicities were cursed with those stereotypes. Similarly, most Blacks are not criminals, yet the group as a whole and their families in particular seem to have in instances suffered long-lasting deterioration as a result of the prison or welfare system or both. The extent and duration of the punishment against Blacks seemed to create a permanent underclass from which many have been unable to escape. Digging into Larry's past, I suddenly wanted to understand better why that was.

I learned about Martin Luther King, Jr., Malcolm X, and the civil rights movements of the sixties. I learned about the Black Panthers and felt a connection in that I now had an uncle who was a past member. What exactly did they do and what did they want? Who were Bobby Seals and Fred Hampton? I learned about the lunch counter conflicts and the protests in Selma. I read James Baldwin's *Go Tell it on the Mountain* and W.E.B. Dubois' original works from the turn of the century. I learned about the reconstruction era and the founding of the Freedmen Schools. I now more deeply admired Harriet Tubman and Fredrick Douglass for their bravery despite the personal risks they incurred.

I understood for the first time that the passage of the Thirteenth, Fourteenth, and Fifteenth Amendments gave Blacks freedom, citizenship, and voting rights, in that order. It was everything theoretically needed on the path to full assimilation into the American culture. Despite this framework, however, the US Supreme Court ruling of "separate but equal" largely erased this progress with acceptance of many Jim Crow laws in the south. Embarrassingly, I realized for the first time that these laws were in effect in much of the south until 1967, the year after I was born. Voting rights were arbitrarily made dependent upon certain locally enacted factors, such as literacy or ability to pay a fee. Interracial marriage was also still illegal in many states until after my birth with the Loving v Virginia case of 1967. If I was uncomfortable bringing a Black girl to an orthopedic dinner in 1995, how did Larry or Joyce feel about having an interracial relationship in 1965? They probably were feeling much more culturally awkward.

I also began looking at Black American cultural icons over the years and the work they had done: Bill Cosby, Michael Jackson, Miles Davis, and Dick Gregory, to name but a few. You can't enter this arena without mentioning Muhammad Ali and all his important contributions to the fight. None of their stories were without blemishes, however—sometimes significant ones. Their white counterparts weren't completely shiny either, but their sins seemed easier to forgive by many. The number of tremendous heroes and motivating actors I stumbled across continued to grow and I finally recognized the magnitude of their work and wove it into my story. I was proud of that history, which now contributed to a larger view of myself.

I could imagine my Black grandfather telling me his story.

"Jack (or Larry, or whatever my name would have been), you'll be living in America but you're not likely to get what they have," he might say. "In a lot of ways, you're living in the land of the enemy. Ever since they brought us here, they have been beating us and making us do their work and dividing our families for their own agenda.

"They killed many of the Indians as well, or marched them across the country into strange desolate lands in order to get rid of them. At some point they freed us, but then continued to oppress us in chain gangs in prison or with lynchings. Fortunately, or not, we didn't even have our own land so they didn't know where to send us. Many of us voluntarily left the South, as their laws were often implemented on very arbitrary and inconsistent grounds.

"They may have given us freedom, citizenship, and the right to vote, but it wasn't the same. We thought this meant that we could then have everything they had here. We thought we could then see, do, and experience everything they saw, did, and enjoyed. We were often taught and began assimilating toward their way of thinking, but it didn't seem to apply to us. They implemented the Jim Crow laws, which effectively took away many of our voting rights and very much restricted the power of our citizenry. They seemed to alter their own laws, which they used like a whip in order to beat us back down again. Their Supreme Court even said it was separate but equal, but it was never equal. Everyone knew that but it was all hush-hush.

"They had relationships with or raped our women and nothing happened to them. If one of our men was caught in a relationship with one of their women, they would be accused of rape and killed. Harper Lee even wrote a book on it, *To Kill a Mockingbird*. That book was just like the young man Emmett Till, who just whistled at a white woman and he was brutally and horribly beaten to death. In the sixties we fought hard and got back some of these rights, but it was never easy. Many of us were killed or jailed during that time. It will never be easy for you either."

Papa taught me fundamentally that this country was here for me to manipulate and control for my own purposes. I could assimilate, follow the rules, and get whatever it was that was due to me for that work and effort. It seemed that the biggest difference that I would have learned from my Black grandfather was that the rules would be constantly used against me.

Their stories were also different fundamentally because Papa *chose* to come here for his family to provide what he could. The Black side of my family was brought here as property, not as men and women with free will. The children of these individuals also became property right out of the womb. The Blacks could learn the rules but then quickly discover that they were often put in place and altered to work against them, not *for* them. All men are created equal, except for the colored ones. The system was in many ways using Blacks to succeed without just compensation, whereas the Italians could use the system for their own personal success.

Italian immigrants could be responsible and use the rewards for their efforts to allow their children to take on roles as police officers, priests, congressmen, or businessmen. Progress has been made, but assimilation seemed to be much more difficult for the Black side of my family because they carried their position in the American hierarchy on the color of their skin and not in their hearts or minds, like the immigrant groups.

This was painful for me to think about. What would it have been like for me if I grew up hearing that this was the story of my people? How would that have affected others' views of me or my view of myself? Why wasn't I taught any of this in school?

Some from my white side would quickly resolve the issue with,

"My family never owned slaves." The general argument is: "Slavery ended 150 years ago so there is no reason to keep bringing it up." Or: "Things are so much better now. Why are they still complaining?"

It didn't seem fair, however, that the Holocaust ended seventy-five years ago yet no one wants to stop bringing *that* up? Jewish people have every right to bring that up. Christians were still mad about the martyrdom of Jesus over two thousand years ago, yet Blacks couldn't bring up Jim Crow laws from 1967? That seemed lacking in empathy, completely disrespectful, and purely racially motivated. I wasn't angry per se, just curious and suddenly much more sympathetic to the other side of my heritage with a very different perspective. Maybe I wasn't angry because life worked out pretty good for me. I realized it could have been so very different with just some very subtle differences in my story or expectations.

I saw myself in Joyce as well, and I could now see how the two battling aspects of the good Jack/bad Jack persona came to be. I honestly couldn't figure out how my two birth parents ever got together in college, but it was the sixties. Who knows what happened back then? They seemed to be complete opposites. I also wasn't really sure who was the good part and who was the bad. I still didn't believe that either part of me or my history was necessarily good or bad, just different. It was good that I worked hard and became an orthopedic surgeon but it was also bad that I spent too much time on my studies and seemed to neglect my relationships.

Of course, the adoption aspect was something unique to me but, if I was honest, I couldn't really put blame purely on the adoption either. Now that I had an understanding of my two parents, a good deal of me had nothing to do with the adoption.

My personality, as I was beginning to understand it, could be somewhat explained by my nature or genetics, my nurture, *plus* a little free will tweaking, independent of the adoption. Adoption wasn't insignificant, however, in that I did feel like I had to work a little harder to fit in and really just figure myself out. The nuanced hardship of that experience was a part of me as well and I was somewhat proud to have survived those battle wounds.

Despite not necessarily knowing the *real me*, I began to develop an understanding that a trifecta of factors went into becoming me. I received life and my nature from Joyce and Larry. I received my nurture from my parents, family, and culture. And I exercised free will under my cultural constraints in deciding what I wanted to do to pursue what I felt was best for me. I really wanted to meet that vanishing twin of mine to see how he would have turned out.

I've read and heard a lot of stories from adoptees in their search for family and how they had become obsessed with the project. It seemed as though I was lucky in how I found my parents, but still, trying to find out more about myself was just as difficult. Ultimately, isn't that what these other adoptees were all trying to do as well? Find themselves? I guess that is probably the importance of having the phrase *Know Thyself* inscribed at the Temple of Delphi. It's not so easy for anyone, adopted or not.

As I educated myself and learned more about African-American history, I began to sincerely appreciate it, become saddened by it, but also be proud of it. There were so many inspiring stories interwoven in the tragedy. I started reconsidering what I thought I knew and was thinking differently myself. I had a sense and felt as though I could better understand how and why Larry may have felt and acted the way he did. It must have been difficult for him. He seemed to be a little bit of a chameleon as well in trying to assimilate. Was he Black or white? Should he marry a Black or white woman? How much was his career affected because some looked at him as Black and some white? Was he held back simply because his success wasn't necessarily tied to being himself, but to this pretend self he was trying to assemble? He did seem to assimilate to a degree by going to college and even marrying a white woman, but not quite totally. I didn't know. I wasn't there, but once again there were infinite possibilities. He really didn't come across to me as a bad guy. He seemed like a reasonably good guy who just found himself in a really difficult situation with more hurdles than the average man of the time.

As I became more comfortable in my pre-Rocco history it made clear all the great things I'd received from my family. I was their prince and they were my everything. My motivation, my support, my love, and confidence in myself all seemed to come from them. They couldn't have children of their own, but my sister and I were a very good plan B. They loved us just as much as any natural parent could, and we didn't seem to fully appreciate it the same way I was appreciating it now. As these emotions of gratitude welled up, I couldn't help feeling horrible for all the ungrateful things I did as a child or lack of expression of my appreciation as an adult. With this newfound self-actualization, I wanted them to know how much I truly was indebted to them for their welcoming love and nurturing all these years. I *had* to tell them of my revelations.

I called my sister, Lisa, to fill her in. I told her of my journey and that her brother was Blacker than we had previously suspected. I also dropped the bomb on her that she now had some competition for best sister. I gave her a heartfelt speech on how lucky we were and what a great job our parents did in raising us. I told her that I was a piece of shit for never having fully realized that and how my love for them had only increased in coming to this realization. She was in full agreement and uncharacteristically silent in pondering these sentiments as well.

"I want to tell Mom and Dad," I said.

"Oh, that is *not* a good idea, Jack," she quickly shot back, trying to break the euphoria.

"No really, Lise. They need to know."

"Jack, you don't understand," she insisted. "They are getting older and can't handle this kind of stress. Dad will flip his lid."

"No, he won't," I persisted. "I think it's kinda funny. All these years they believed the nuns that we were Italian but it makes sense that we aren't. You are probably part Black too, you know.

That's probably why the kids all called you Aunt Jemima growing up."

"Yeah, no shit. Probably. But I'm never going to find out," she assured me.

"Do you want to?" I asked.

"Kinda, but I couldn't do that to Mom and Dad," she admitted.

"So I'm the bad guy?" I asked.

"No, Kari-Ann is. But you still can't tell them," she said.

"She's not the bad guy either. It was true whether I found out about it or not. She just got the ball rolling. Lise, really, I'm coming home for Father's Day and I want to tell Mom and Dad. It will be fine," I reassured her. "You have to trust me on this one. I have appreciated this whole process and want them to be a part of it. It'll be fine. I promise."

"Well, you know I'll be there for you," she said. "But I still don't think it's a good idea."

"I know," I agreed. "But Lise, I think we need this. It'll be fine."

I wasn't exactly sure what to expect, but flying by the seat of my pants was kind of my specialty at this point. So I had no doubt it was all going to turn out better than I could ever have imagined, just like almost everything else in my life.

CHAPTER 10
...AND PAPA?

IN 1989, I WROTE A POEM ENTITLED "WHO IS THIS MAN?"

Now, I am not a *poet* and definitely *know it*, but from the time I wrote this little passage it has intrigued me. I really didn't know where it came from. It seemed important and profound to me when I wrote it but I wasn't quite sure what it meant.

It was the summer between my first and second years of medical school. My Erie classmates and I were driving to another friend's summer lake house to learn how to sailboard. I don't remember exactly what was going on in my head at the time but as I sat in the passenger seat watching the trees fly by, the monotony of the road had me in a trance. Suddenly, for no particular reason, these words started forming in my brain. I hadn't set out to write a poem on that trip but it just started happening.

During the school year, the intensity of the work and the level of competition amongst my classmates put me on constant high alert with near maniacal focus. My heart and mind were also tangled in a whirlwind of cultural crosscurrents trying to determine how to survive this dust bowl of class warfare and confusion. This relaxing trip and sunny day seemed to help all of those emotions spill out from my psyche.

I grabbed a scrap piece of paper and pen and started transcribing the thoughts. I was curious to see where this was going. Within thirty minutes I'd finished, and was pleased with the fact that it mostly rhymed and seemed to convey some coherent thoughts. Later, I typed it up in a fancy font and even laminated it for posterity. I've kept it with me ever since.

Who Is This Man?
Am I the man who loves to sing,
Or just sit and talk about anything?
Or am I the man who is quiet and shy,
Has plenty of feelings but would never cry?
Am I the man who could play for days
And have fun in so many different ways?
Or am I the man who worries too much,
about love and war and life and such?
Am I the man who is caring and giving,
Lets others live and does his own living?
Or am I the man who is selfish and cruel,
Hates to listen and loves to rule?
Who is this man that I call me?
Is he something more or just what you see?
When will it end, this struggle for self?
Will I find it with love, success, or great wealth?
How will I know when I've reached my peak?
Am the man I should be, not worthless and weak?
Maybe I'm beneath all these masks I display.
I can only keep going and live for today.
I must keep trying the best that I can,
But can't ever stop asking, just who is this man?

I had no idea who I was and couldn't even see myself and my characteristics clearly in my surroundings. I seemed to be lurking just beneath any number of disguises I would change as needed to fit the occasion.

Today, I recognize the feelings in that poem as being very directly initiated by the birth separation and adoption phenomenon. Even though I didn't know it, the reverberations of that relinquishment had never really stopped for me. At that time, however, I had no understanding of the adoption fog that was surrounding me. Over the years, I had become accustomed to feeling on the outside of experiences but was constantly trying to get to the inside. My whole life had been that way growing up. Medical school was no different. I wasn't going to allow anyone to know what I was thinking because I myself didn't know what I was thinking. I was often waiting to see what everyone else thought. Years earlier I also learned how to skillfully keep everyone away from my soft inner core, including myself.

That wasn't all bad, however. That level of insecurity constantly provided me with the necessary adrenaline and cortisol to fly through the world, with all of its problems just rolling off me like water on a duck. My intensity level was typically on high and the idea of slowing down to smell a rose or two was, in my mind, a luxury I couldn't afford. I have to admit a lot of that drive and inability to relax was in large part responsible for my academic progress. That level of dedication very much describes a recipe for success in the professional world. It wasn't until years later that it became obvious the negative role this insecurity played in the neglect of my emotional or personal relationships. I did almost everything for other people or what I suspected they wanted me to do given my abilities. For whatever reason, at that time, my methods seemed to be working, so why would I want anyone to change it?

Looking back, I can quite easily see how that struggle for self could be tied to the trauma of being separated from my mother at birth. For the longest time I didn't know I had any trauma in my life. I would have denied it till I was blue in the face. I might still deny it now, but experiencing how useless I was as a father to my newborn children at times made me appreciate the maternal bond even more. I never had access to that. Seeing all those children in the Madagascar orphanages also affected me so deeply. I could seemingly recognize the struggle in their behavior and feel their pain so much deeper than I ever imagined.

My early years growing up *were* a very solid foundation; it just wasn't necessarily *my* foundation. Without knowing myself or having mirrors around that reflected me, I couldn't ever really see me in my world. The subconscious minds of many adoptees seem to sense that discrepancy, like a little chick that has imprinted on a cat. I thought much of my past was great but truly my connection to it was only partial; I wasn't authentic. My deeper brain seemed to somehow know I was pretending.

Often in the struggle to belong, the last person I worried about was myself. Where did my allegiance lie on the day I wrote that poem? I was trying to figure it out but also trying to maintain "Jack" as I committed myself to becoming "Dr. Rocco." I sensed deeply that I had to choose between the two but realized quickly that others wanted Dr. Rocco. The medical admissions board did not accept Jack, or if they did, it was only on the condition that he become Dr. Rocco. I was struggling with whether I could ever fully cut Jack out of the deal. I couldn't do that, could I? Jack was too folksy, too uncertain, and way too Italian. *Fuggedaboutit.* Dr. Rocco needed to be more serious, more commanding, and have much less poofy hair. All that was required of me to complete the transition was to comply and everything would be just fine. "Trust us," the board seemed to say.

The oldest neurons in my brain both personally and evolutionarily, however, were debating amongst themselves when they asked, *Didn't you already do that once before years ago with Little Larry when you forgot all about him and replaced him with Jack?* I couldn't remember. Or rather, I could remember but just couldn't recall.

When I read the poem now, it says to me, *You got this. You don't really know what you're doing or even who you are but you know what to do to survive. You've made it this far. Right now, you're still pretending, but you will eventually figure it out. You will have to maintain the wisdom to realize it's all a game. Keep playing but don't ever lose the drive to keep looking for yourself. You may need to know that man just in case he is able to escape someday.*

That someday had arrived, and Little Larry was scratching from the inside trying to get out.

It was Father's Day weekend 2018 and I was in Erie. We'd had a family picnic with the whole crew earlier in the day at Waldameer Park and Water World. This is your classic small-town amusement park and has been an Erie landmark since 1896. It has been around for so long that everyone in the family pretty much grew up there, attending innumerable school trips and various other events. Their slogan is "You're Gonna Love It!"—and we did.

The day was winding down and we drove back to my parents' house. Sitting in front of the garage behind our house, my father and I opened a bottle of wine. Three-fourths of the way through the bottle, Lisa arrived. This was exactly how I wanted it. It was just the four of us, as it had been for so long in the beginning. No spouses, no children, no other family members. It was just as it was when we were twelve and ten, sitting at the table together with our parents.

I had learned so much more about myself since reuniting with Joyce. That knowledge had vastly increased over the past few months in learning about Larry's side of the family. I felt great about the progress I was making. I was who I was and was personally and fully accepting of it. I was proud of the process and journey I was on and felt more complete than I had at any other point in my life. Being able to finally share these details with the people I loved and respected the most was exciting. Bringing my parents on board was the final step in having others accept my revelations as well.

In retrospect, it really wasn't fair of me to drop this in their lap without warning. I had been hiding and digesting this information for eleven years and hadn't handled it so gracefully myself. I had come to an acceptance, but it wasn't without a great deal of private soul-searching and reflection. Just like my surprise proposal to Kari-Ann at the family dinner table, it seemed as though my MO involved some stealthy Trojan Horse plan—how to start from the outside and work my way in. Jack could never just walk up and knock on the door as himself. How would that possibly work? I was doing it again. As a result of my pathologic habits, I didn't give my parents the slightest warning as to what was in store.

I oozed with confidence and self-realization. I was calm and ready to tell my parents the whole story. Lisa was still *not* on board, yet in my determination all I had heard her say was, "I'll be there for you, but something, something, something." This was going to be great for all of us. I was accustomed to my new truth and proud of the work I had done in preparation. I was ready to present it to them in an unembarrassed fashion. I had spent over a decade sneaking around behind their backs and I was good with everything I had discovered. I wanted to end the secrecy. They were going to be so pleased. I was a grown man now. I was mentally, physically, and emotionally prepared to do this. Or was I?

"You want some wine?" I asked Lisa.

"No, I can't because of my medication," she replied.

"Oh yeah, I forgot," I said as I looked at the nearly empty bottle we had on the table. "Well, I think we need another bottle anyway."

I was getting butterflies in my stomach and realized I was going to need a little more liquid courage for the conversation we were about to have. As I stood up to go get another bottle, Lisa declared she had to use the bathroom and followed me into the house.

"Are you really going to do this?" she asked once we were inside.

"Yes, of course," I told her.

"I don't know, Jack," she replied.

I understood what she was saying. I was just as nervous but I couldn't show that. I really couldn't take it any longer. This had gone on for too long and the secret I carried with me was killing me. There was no need for the secrecy anymore. We were all grown-ups and there was no reason why we couldn't talk about Lisa and I being adopted. It was not embarrassing anymore. It was a part of us and we had done just fine with it. We were better than fine; we were great. Given the reading I had done and what I had witnessed in the orphanages of Madagascar, I was proud of that.

I wanted my parents to hear what I had been through. I wanted them to hear the story of the blind date and realize that everyone was lied to during this process over the years. It was common. I wanted them to be proud of me that I had walked into the cave, faced my demons, and come out alive. Despite the hurdles, I realized all the great things that adoption did for us. I wanted to celebrate the life and family we were able to enjoy. I wanted them to be proud of the job *they* did. They were great parents and we turned out great. They should have been proud this whole time. They honestly should have been standing in their front yard with a big sign that said, "We raised these two beautiful children to be great adults and they weren't even really ours...Damn it!"

For many understandable reasons, all three members of the adoption triad struggle. It is absolutely tragic for everyone and lies often seem to be necessary when dealing with young children. I wasn't naïve, but we could all stop pretending. I couldn't live with myself if I went back home without sharing. I had been riding on an emotional rollercoaster for a long time and wanted off. This was happening. All I had to do was tell the story without hesitancy or doubt and it would be fine.

I can't say I practiced word for word what I was going to say, but I had become so comfortable with it over the past several years, I wasn't worried. I would start with my main purpose which was to thank them and tell them how much I loved them for everything they had done. Then I would tell them the backstory as I had recently discovered it. I would move forward chronologically so that they could enjoy the journey as I traveled it. This should be easy. It was showtime!

"We'll be fine, Lise."

"Okay, but it's all on you," Lisa told me begrudgingly as we headed to the backyard.

Once outside, I filled my glass. All my backstage jitters welled up as I looked at my audience sitting there, completely clueless as to what they were about to experience.

"The kids had a blast at the park today," Lisa began, maybe hoping I would forget or become sidetracked.

"Oh, they did, hun! It was a beautiful day," my mother confirmed.

The conversation continued until there was a brief millisecond of pause during which I looked at Lisa with a subtle glance that said, *Now?* Just like when we were children, our mother knew instantly that something was up.

"What's going on?" she asked.

I looked at Lisa again, desperately wanting her to take the lead and save me all the trouble I'd so boldly downplayed not even five minutes earlier. I was reminded of the feeling I had as I went in on that wasp nest despite her warnings to the contrary. She just calmly shot me her open-eyed stare with raised eyebrows look that said, *Well, go ahead. You dragged me here for this.*

It still wasn't easy. I hesitated for way too long and it was starting to get uncomfortable. I didn't do well with pregnant pauses and forgot my lines.

"Well," I stammered while instinctively regressing to my childhood ways of looking for someone else to blame. "About fourteen years ago, before Sophia was born, Kari-Ann asked me if I wanted to find my birth parents."

"Aw, Jack," my mother let out with that characteristic sense of disappointment.

I reflexively tried to clear my guilt. "Ma, I told her no. But then she said, 'Don't you think we should know your medical history?' But I told her, 'No, not really. I never knew and she'll know that I'm healthy.' Anyway, after a few months she said, 'If I get the paperwork, will you sign it?' So I eventually did."

They knew what was coming. My mother dejectedly looked at my sister as if I was confessing to serial murders and said, "You're not doing this too, are you?"

Lisa quickly and defensively replied, "No!" She wanted to put as much distance between the two of us as possible. She let it be known that she would *never* do anything as stupid as what her brother was now admitting to.

I realized, embarrassed, that Lisa was right again, and I could hear her denial imply, *I told you so!* just like when we were kids. It was too late, as I had already been poking at the wasp nest for some time and a confession was necessary.

My father sat even more eerily quiet than usual.

Oh shit! This is going terribly wrong, I thought. I wanted a do-over. I felt myself starting to dodge and scramble in the gauntlet and realized I just had to quickly get to the point so they would understand my conclusion of appreciation. There were no do-overs. I had to push on. This was a story worth telling. I restarted, trying to stay focused and calm.

"Well, about eleven years ago the state called me back and told me they found my mother," I said, listening to my own voice quiver as everyone sat in deafening silence. "So we eventually met, but my father had died the year before, in 2006. In January, I looked for my father's side of the family and met a bunch of cousins, aunts, and his only surviving brother. I found out I have four half siblings—all living in North Carolina, no more than three hours from me."

My eyes darted around as I watched each of them slowly lower their heads into their hands so I couldn't see the tears starting to flow. My quivering increased. I had to get to the point.

"I know you don't like to hear that, but I just want you to know that it made me appreciate you guys so much more and realize everything you did for us," I said. "I just wanted to let you know how grateful I am for everything. Lisa and I lived with it, Ma, and just took for granted what you both did for us. It turns out, my birth parents were just regular kids who went to college in Mansfield. They were both studying to be teachers and he played football and she got pregnant and that's just what they did back then. It really isn't a big deal."

I tried to reassure them it didn't matter, but at this point I wished I had listened to Lisa. Clearly this was a big deal to my parents.

I was delusional to think this was going to go any other way than the way it was unfolding. Somewhere in the euphoric mania of my distorted reality, I'd thought this was going to be fine. I was so determined to will this into a happy ending that I never imagined I would be crying. By the time I finished my highly shortened and scrambled story, everyone was sobbing.

I put my head into my hands and stared at the concrete as well. Couldn't they see that I loved them all along and even more now? I was older now and had children of my own. I had failed as a husband and father and was amazed at how relatively easy my parents made it look. My kids would never understand how short I came up in my goal of giving them everything I had and more. I thought my parents were going to be so proud of me for coming to the realization of their greatness. Why weren't they impressed?

This really wasn't such a big deal. In contrast, my marriage separation *was* a big deal because my kids were still young and we were now living seven hundred miles apart. I had ruined my marriage and that was my fault. I thought I had my flimsy unexplainable reasons, but what I just told them was *not* a big deal in my eyes. I thought it made for a funny or interesting story of how it all came to be.

My father was fully red-faced and shaking as he desperately tried to hold it all in. I hated seeing my father cry. It happened so infrequently and was so contrary to his usual character that this suddenly became an even bigger deal than I could have ever imagined.

"Jack, all that stuff you just told us," he said. "We already knew that."

Now I knew he didn't know about the search for my birth parents and all he really knew was that they had been two young college kids who couldn't afford to raise a child.

But you don't know the rest of it, I thought to myself. I had barely told them anything at that point. My current revelation was really not much more than the same story I had been told since I was three or four years old.

"Five people went to their graves with that secret," he continued.

I was struck. *What secret?* I hadn't even gotten to the secret yet. I never mentioned anything about Larry's race. I was saving that until the end, allowing for the initial shock to settle in first. *What five people?* There was a pause as I thought through what had just happened.

"You mean Uncle Joe, Aunt B, Aunt Jill, Grama, and Papa?" I asked.

"Yeah," he replied. "Before we even brought you home, we had to tell all the grown-ups in the family about you. The nuns made us tell everyone so that they all knew."

Knew what? I thought. *What is he saying?* It was like a judo take-down I didn't see coming. Suddenly the tables were turned, and I was on the mat looking up at the ceiling lights without the advantage of the wisdom I thought I had.

I came out of my Trojan horse. "You mean that my father was Black?" I slowly questioned.

"Yes," he affirmed.

What? My brain was glitching. There were so many thoughts and visions racing through my mind. I couldn't say another word. I couldn't think another thought.

The conversation quickly fell to silence as only sobs and sniffles filled the air.

As the tears were drying, and my brain was rebooting, we all just sat and processed our own thoughts independent of one another. I can't tell you how much time passed but it seemed like hours. I looked over to Lisa during the silence. She had nothing to say either. She was just as shocked and speechless as I was.

I had been blaming the nuns this whole time for duping us, but it turned out the nuns were innocent and it was my family who made the decision to not tell me of my mixed race. I hope God forgives me for blaming the nuns all these years. My conversation with St. Peter at the Pearly Gates is going to take a lot longer than I expected. We may have to go into a private conference room or something.

My war plan, if you will, was an offensive one. I would come in, tell my story, and let them know how much I loved them for what they did. I'd pass out Hershey's bars and go on to further win their hearts and minds in this discovery campaign. It was even a surprise attack, yet somehow, I was just as effectively neutralized in a quagmire. How could they possibly have defeated me so efficiently?

And the weapon! Where in the hell did they get that weapon?

...and Papa? I thought.

Really? Everyone knew? I'd expected this was going to be the end but now the thoughts had to cycle all over again.

They didn't tell me?

...and Papa? Good god, not Papa! He was in on it too? He never let on? We spent more time together than anyone.

I was suddenly transported back in time to my younger life. The moments from years ago flashed before my eyes. I mowed his grass and shoveled his snow, painted his house, and worked almost every day in the basement building grandfather clock cabinets during the summers. I gave him full credit for teaching me the early skills of working with my hands and thinking in numbers, precision, and three dimensions—so valuable in allowing me to become what I thought was a pretty good orthopedic surgeon. Those qualities allowed me to help so many people over so many years and make a good living for my family.

I went with him on jobs to fix things for family or install elaborate fireplace facades for some fairly wealthy people. I ate so many meals in their house, by myself and with the whole family. There were so many holidays, so many picnics, and so many deep conversations solving all of the world's problems. We spent endless days fishing Lake Erie, Walnut Creek, and the lagoons on Presque Isle, where I caught *him* with a fish hook as I was trying to cast. We spent all that time together and he never gave me a clue?

Well, there was that one time when I was fourteen or fifteen and he told me as I sat in the front passenger seat of his car, "Jack, suck in your lips." Was he trying to tell me that I was starting to look Black because I had big lips or something? Were my lips bigger than normal during those awkward days of puberty and maturation?

In those few moments, the whole of my life passed before my eyes, but now instead of Jack in the scenes, Little Larry was the child. Unexpectedly, as an unintended consequence, the uncovering of the systemic lie finally allowed me to see *myself* playing in the backyard or sitting in my seat at the table. I saw a small, very light-skinned Black boy getting out of the car and running down the stairs. I heard soft whispers through windows while we were all outside riding our bikes. *See, no one can tell.* I felt private thoughts forming at the most random of times. *He doesn't really even look Black.*

That was there all this time? They saw who I was but just didn't want to tell me?

So much of the basic foundation of my life was a lie, and I'd sensed it but still went along with it. If it was all no big deal then why couldn't I know? If I was fake this whole time, had my achievements and life been fake as well?

...and Papa? The words bounced around my brain like a pinball as an unbelievable realization too heavy at the time to fully appreciate. *Papa too?*

This had not gone as planned. *Really?*

Papa was my biggest mentor, my best friend, my motivator, and provided the vast majority of fuel needed for my success. Then again, my success wasn't just tied to fuel. I was also a naturally built chassis and engine and computer navigation system.

I wrote his eulogy with such emotional depth that the process of writing it drained me for months. I cried repeatedly in the process over the brilliance of its beauty. I used Shel Silverstein's book *The Giving Tree,* as an example of our relationship. He was my tree and I was his boy.

That eulogy was such an enormous tribute to his life and everyone felt I delivered it with such perfection that we all wished he had been there to hear it. I wished I had told him all of it before he died. In that final act of thanks to him, I was able to prove to myself and everyone else the deep love, appreciation, and understanding of his life's mission even though I was a "recycled" kid. Despite having never written a eulogy before, I was still able to capture what everyone loved about him. I was the recycled child whom he never treated as recycled. He made me believe I was the chosen one, the special child, his apprentice put on this planet to carry on his legacy. Everyone else in the room felt the same way about him. They were chosen as well, special and put on this planet for a reason. Everyone was special to him and they all knew it.

I thought we were tight. *But he was in on it?*

While I sensed the whole time that I was on the outside looking in, I still did everything I could to fit in. I thought I had them all fooled. I thought they forgot I was adopted. *I* forgot I was adopted for a good long while myself. I thought my chameleon colors were so good, but it seemed I was the one most fooled.

I tried to add in a few more details after everything settled down, but they didn't want to hear any of it. I realized that I had embarrassed them in unwinding the illusion they had created for our benefit and I felt horrible for it.

I knew none of this was funny, but in my idealized eighties sitcom ending I envisioned us all laughing over how stupid I was and how well the prank had played out all these years. Laughing over things like that was how we always coped. Aunt B's disability, Uncle Armand's shortness, and Uncle Lenny's Polishness: nothing was off the table when a good laugh was the payoff. We loved making fun of each other and ourselves. None of that happened. We dropped the conversation and eventually went to bed.

The following morning Lisa and I were still mulling over the situation. She seemed to be slowly coming to my side of the argument that this needed to come out and maybe felt more enlightened herself. It was shocking that they kept this secret for so long, but I think we both understood their intentions. I sent her a funny Bitmoji text with my caricature on his knees, reaching to the sky with the left hand and the right clutching his heart. The caption read NOOOOOOOOO. I added, *I still can't believe that I'm Black and you're not. I want a recount!* She replied with a snidely confident, *LMBAO!!! (Laughing My Black Ass Off) Oh no, no recount.*

I tried again to help my parents see the humor in it the next day. A group of the cousins and I went golfing with my father and Uncle Armand the next morning. Uncle Armand was always the jokester. We always laughed about the most ridiculous things to make light of life's cruelties and injustices. Our hardships were always followed by a punch line. "We'll laugh about this someday," was our mantra.

I was still waiting for the comic relief to sneak into the dialogue. I would have felt better about it if someone else besides me was looking for the levity in the situation. Certainly Uncle Armand would help my father understand that this really was kind of funny.

"Hey, Uncle Armand, the cat's out of the bag!" I blurted on the third tee box that day.

"What cat?" he replied.

"The black cat," I cleverly retorted in the spur of the moment.

"You never asked," he just as cleverly shot back.

No one continued the conversation. They seriously weren't playing with this issue and I dropped it too. We finished our round, and I got in the car and drove back to North Carolina, staring and thinking for the next nine hours as the white lines passed by my window.

Really? I "never asked?" Was this some sort of secret Masonic society or something and the key resided in me just asking? Oh, I see, it was all my fault. That's ridiculous. How was I supposed to know that?

As I reflected on what had just happened, I knew I *had* to be mad at someone over all of this. I was part Black my whole life, everyone knew, and no one thought that would be important to tell me? Come on, man! That could have come up a million times over the years. As I drove, I was waiting for the anger, but I was just numb. I started looking for the responsible party. My parents were the natural first suspects in that they had intentionally kept things from me all these years. Papa was also a good choice since he was the oldest and should have known better. Then there were Joyce and Larry, who started this whole mess. I was also a grown man myself now and my rosy view on the world had long lost its hue. How did I not figure that out sooner? I was living in my brain this whole time; I knew what was going on in there. *I* should have figured that one out. As a result, I also looked in the mirror quite a bit. Ignorance is no excuse for the law and I certainly wasn't a completely innocent victim. I could have figured it out but didn't *want* to figure it out. The anger never came.

With the amount of reality I had under my belt, I knew there wasn't just one individual responsible, or even or a limited group. It wasn't just my family who had awkward feelings about my mixed race. There was an untold number of responsible parties over thousands of years who had aversion to people not like themselves. The world has changed, and being mixed-race is not such a big deal anymore. Larry seemed to have an issue with it as well. In my experience, when you're mixed-race, it's almost as if people want to know which side you're on. I couldn't always say, and for some reason no one really liked that.

I should have been told as much as possible about my history earlier in my life, ideally at the same time I was told of my adoption. Then again, I can't really say I blame my family for hiding that from me and everyone else. Let's face it, during the early years of my life, it was risky to let that information out. I potentially would have been teased and may have had to kick a few asses, like Armand, in the process.

My *self* was, in essence, sacrificed due to society's discomfort in dealing with who I was.

Various cultures are all so different, but the natural humanity is also easy to see if you just take time to look for it. There is no reason why we shouldn't all be able to celebrate every percentage point of our genetic makeup fully adding up to 100 percent. No one is pure anything. Hiding those secrets or refusing to see color because *you* believe those *different* from you are somehow flawed is a poison, which only serves to erode the body in which it is contained. Those thoughts will eventually get out and damage the vessel in the process. The understanding of our commonality can be taught or nurtured to be better incorporated into our interactions. Instead, exclusion and fear seem to be our preferred path of least resistance.

In seeing my parents' reaction to my confession, I felt their pain and knew they were ashamed, and too overwhelmed to even try and explain. They never got defensive or lashed out at me. They were hurt just as much as I was and didn't even want to joke about it. I knew they would never do anything to hurt me even if it was unintended. They were clearly trying to protect me from a monster they knew existed, but were confused as to what to do about it. They couldn't stop it but felt the best thing they could do was to take me away from it and fill their own desires as well. Everyone at that time told them adoption was a win-win scenario. My experience *was* great for me in so many ways, but it takes a fool to believe that erasing a person, transferring them into another culture, and pretending that everything is normal will ever come off without a hitch. It's not that simple.

So is that their biggest crime? Not wanting me to be discriminated against? Our family didn't talk publicly about anything potentially embarrassing that might expose an Achilles heel of weakness. They didn't want me to stand out, be picked on, or bullied. In those days and even today, they certainly weren't the only ones with these limitations of experience and culture. We never even had the "sex talk." They left that for me to learn in health class and on the streets. How did I expect them to have the unwanted child or race relations talks? Things were not as transparent in much of the twentieth century as they are now. *Everyone* was in a fog and still is to a great extent. My parents and Papa didn't know any more about solving it than anyone else. So that would definitely be their defense, and I think the verdict would be up for grabs depending on the racial mix of the jurors.

In a perfect world, I do think they should have told me at some point. Understanding the slowly changing racial environment over the course of my life, there were plenty of opportunities. But things don't change for everyone at the same pace. I can't say at what age I think that would have been best handled. Once the lie was set in place, each age would have carried with it a certain degree of risk and benefit. I think it was probably the fact that my life seemed to be going so well and I was notoriously sensitive to change that kept my parents from speaking. Honestly, at every age they probably figured, "Why mess things up now?" At some point they probably forgot about it, just as I did prior to Kari-Ann initiating the search for Joyce.

I still wanted to be angry and I was but at who? What was so wrong about me that it had to be hidden all these years? I've thought about this a lot, but am I angry with anyone in particular? I absolutely am not. It's been said that no single raindrop feels responsible for the flood. It just seems as though the phenomenon of subdividing people into various categories of good and bad is a part of the very ether we deal with on a day-to-day basis.

Most of us have, at some point, been on both the receiving and giving ends of unfair judgment. My situation is no different. It is an inescapable truth that everyone lies and no one likes being lied to. This is especially true when the lie is long-standing and has undeniably and significantly altered the one and only life you were given.

All the lies of my life are an inseparable element of my being that I cannot eliminate, no matter how hard I try. It doesn't matter if they made my life better or worse, there is still a sense of longing and loss for that life that never was. Being angry also doesn't change the gratitude for what I've received or the sadness for what I've lost. I've come to realize I am allowed to be angry, grateful, *and* sorrowful. These are not binary either/or emotions. You can have many simultaneously. It is what it is.

Two days after Father's Day, my mother called. "Your father just wants everything to go back to the way it was," she told me.

That was the last time we ever talked about it. Go back to the way it was? Okay, that's what we did, and it wasn't hard because we had pretended for so long that I knew what to do. I just had to publicly continue with the status quo. Being accustomed to compartmentalizing, learning more about my story really didn't change anything with us. It may have changed things for me quite a bit, but there was no reason for it to change anything with our family—and for the most part, it hasn't.

The one way it did change everything, however, was in making me realize that my parents were human as well. It forced me to accept the unusual circumstances they were placed in as adoptive parents of a mixed-race child in the sixties. They were much stronger and rebellious than I ever knew and that gave them a strong quality of super humanity that I never saw in them before. Just like my superhuman experience of celebrating that patient's death, this didn't look so good on them either. It didn't take away from the fact that what they did was remarkable. Being so close, my family can't keep *anything* a secret, and they all managed to keep this a secret for over fifty years. They never explained, never complained, and never blamed, they just did it.

I had read enough about adoption dynamics over the years to empathize with how they felt. Not being able to have children of their own, they wanted us to be their real children and they wanted to be our real parents—and we were, and they were, as much as possible. As great as it was, and it was great, it was impossible for them to share my kinky hair, bubble butt, academic interests, and traumatic experience of being relinquished by my mother. It wasn't any of our faults, and we all understood that, but no one had the courage to ever mention it.

The lies I discovered on my journey really didn't change all the good we shared.

In a way I was greatly relieved because it put an end to eleven years of curiosity, discovery, and sneaking around without them knowing. It's just absurd that I had to jump through so many hoops to realize I was a "real kid" all along. I was a real kid whose birth parents didn't marry and buy into the American Dream of 1966. My parents didn't adopt me to hurt me, and clearly they all thought I was better off not knowing. Maybe they hoped it would all go away before I got old enough to realize.

I couldn't get my parents to explain because they were never prepared to explain themselves. They really just didn't have the words to express what was going on in their minds. It was a lot to digest and much heavier than any of us ever recognized. I know and love them enough to understand that. I know they chose not to tell me to protect me, and I understand how difficult it would have been to just bring it up out of the blue like I did. Everything was going great in my life. Why mess with me?

My mother had told me on more than one occasion growing up that I was sensitive. She was right. I am sensitive, even though I try not to show it. Was that the code they used back in the day for what might now be called the adoptive personality syndrome? Probably. I was a freaking ugly duckling given up by my mother at birth! Of course I was going to be sensitive. It wasn't really necessary for them to throw another monkey wrench into my life when I was running so fast and efficiently around the track of life's success. My mother truly understood me better than I understood myself in a lot of ways. She was absolutely correct from the nurture side of my being; she just couldn't understand that the natural side of me already knew the secret. I really couldn't muster up anger at anyone in particular over it but it did make me think deeply about it, repeatedly. Remember, I'm sensitive like that.

I get all that, but how do I forgive my best friend, Papa, for not having had the wisdom to know that I should have had access to who I was both genetically and culturally? Those two elements of me were missing from the start of my life, and my family was really only able to give me the cultural aspect. I was raised by them so well I wasn't really aware that I was missing a natural element for so long. It was a factor that I nonetheless did well without, culturally. Not every adoptee has the same luck. Some suffer through more and are much more severely affected by it. For me, it was a wonderful, nurturing culture but all this "blank slate" nonsense? No child is a blank slate on the day they are born. The lie that I was a blank slate who could be molded into anything they wanted with the proper nurturing just wasn't true. That narrative had been going on from long before their birth and they just went along with the story they were told. Locking away my original birth certificate and family history legally made me someone new, but I was still and always would be what God or nature intended me to be.

I've learned enough about genetic and psychological evolution over the years to know that our cultural history is just as much a part of our initial core as is our potential height or eye color at the moment of conception. Some of our features are altered by our environment; others are not.

Having my own children confirmed that to me even more. Sophia was Sophia and James was James, in essence, from the moment they each were born. They have their own personalities and both of them are an absolute continuation of the infants they were. Kari-Ann and I can help them to see themselves in us and they will continue to look at us with intense scrutiny as they grow. We are their mirrors. They see themselves in us, and us in them. We can teach them whatever we want, but our behavior and lives are a greater example of who we are to them than we can ever explain. I had plenty of very good mirrors in my life but none of them allowed me to see the uniqueness or ordinariness of myself. I could only see my family, and I tried to be like them—all of them—good or bad. It's what adopted kids do.

This whole Father's Day debacle, in retrospect, affected me much less than the blind date incident. I was better prepared for it in that I had found my biologic family prior to the confrontation. I quickly realized my parents couldn't travel with me on this journey, but I had something to fall back on. After the blind date and for the longest time beyond that, I had nothing to fall back on. It was a limitless abyss below me. With this incident, I had a trampoline made of Joyce, Larry, and the truth below me. It really wasn't much of a fall.

I was also older, had been around the world, and had seen quite a few absolutely horrible displays of humanity in the process. This was a sin of omission, made by my parents for my benefit. This was not so bad. Racism is definitely an evil in this world, especially if it's slung at you. They protected me from it and I get that. I hate that our civil society still has to deal with it. The fight against it will and should go on. The journey I went on has made me more aware of the depths and significance of it. I understood why they would want to protect me from it.

I do believe that Uncle Joe would have recognized that value of self over society and told me the truth. That revelation certainly would have changed me in the process for "good" and "bad." He was probably the only member of the family who would have understood that, having been adopted himself. Unfortunately, his brain tumor got the best of him and he never had the chance.

Papa, my parents, and the whole family truly believed they were doing the right thing in protecting me from society and the truth. They didn't know how American society would take me and, as immigrants, we weren't "from here." In many ways they weren't wrong. They loved this country and went along with all the generally accepted beliefs of the time. Papa wasn't stupid, and he knew how the rules were set up here from the time he stepped onto America's shores. He came to America during the peak of the eugenics movement and lived through Hitler's implementation of it. Italians were one of the groups considered to be defective at the time. Anyone who wasn't absolutely perfectly bred and trained in the western standard were on that list as well. He wasn't a guy who rocked the boat, and he wasn't about to let anyone know about any potential targets in his family. He assimilated and blindly followed America's rules—even if he disagreed with them

—but that was a double-edged sword. He was always "good" and compliant and maybe understood the value in Semper Gumby.

My family wasn't racist for not wanting to tell me of my ethnic and racial heritage, but the results were the same. The culture of secrecy and shame was trying to erase a part of me. It was trying to cover up and hide the inconvenient part of me that wasn't quite ready to be fully accepted into the American fabric of 1966. Thankfully, the world continues to evolve, as those uncomfortable truths don't want to stay trapped underground forever. There was an unintended consequence and pleasant surprise that came from having the lie out of the way. My nurture, nature, and free will decisions were now placed into a new context within a more accurate history and a societal value placed on each. As a result, I could finally, and quite literally, see myself and my life much more clearly.

CHAPTER 11
THE MIRROR

IT'S BEEN JUST A FEW YEARS SINCE THAT FAMILY CONVERSATION ABOUT my birth parents. So much has changed, but so much has also stayed the same. I still frequently visit Erie and try to stop and see as many people as I can—even if only briefly. I can never visit as much as I would like but it seems to be much more important than ever to visit, especially given the pandemic of 2020. Since I work in a hospital and my family is in an older, more vulnerable position, I'm a high-risk encounter for them. The isolation, the fear, and all the political and racial discord made us long for time together and appreciate the good times of the past and future memories even more.

My parents, aunts, and uncles all live in the same houses they did when I was growing up. When I visit, even from my social distance, I still find myself falling right back into my same role as Jack, and I love it. My mother and father have taken over the job of feeding the family during the major holidays. Not everyone makes it: there are so many more now and everyone has naturally moved in various directions. There are different children crawling on the floor and refusing to eat their dinner, but fundamentally we are all the same and tightly connected. They are special, chosen, and some recycled, but they are all loved. I can relate intimately to that.

The chain to the past has not been broken and should not be severed in the future.

When I drive the streets of Erie, I notice that the air is cleaner, as the forges and foundries are all closed and smoke no longer blows into the air. The empty rusted-out buildings sit like ancient sarcophagi lining the railroad tracks just down the street from my parents' house. Hagarty's Bar and Grill, "Home of the Six-Pack," is not so crowded anymore given the environment and the fact that blue-collar work ain't what it used to be.

For the longest time, given where I came from—adoption, this town, and my parents—to where I ended up, I thought I was a self-made man. That was my own stupid lie for which I am undeniably guilty. Certainly, I am not alone in that delusion. I never did it all on my own, but my parents and family wouldn't take any of the credit they deserved either. "Oh, shut up, Jack," they would say. "We didn't do nothing." But that's bullshit!

My parents gave me the opportunity to believe in magic even if it was at times pretend, yet find inner joy and gratitude in being a part of something that really was wonderful and highly imperfect simultaneously. All that pretending and whistling past the grave-yard worked, and a good attitude was the best thing they could have given me. Being optimistic and eventually laughing at every-thing helps.

That was my experience and despite whatever struggles I had in the meantime, *for me* it was worth the price. Many adoptees aren't so lucky. No one is really lucky in that situation, but many have it worse. Of course, it isn't a competition, but people always compare. I'm not saying they should hold onto their victimhood either, but it is a highly complex situation and the relinquished child particularly needs help moving on and dealing with the issues lingering in their subconscious. The ripples of those initial struggles can definitely magnify over the years.

Somewhere deep in the inner core of my humanity, I was always traumatized by that loss. The separation from my mother, extended family, and history left me floating in a void of time and space without a tether. I was just really glad to have been where I was and my family was glad to have me. The Roccos helped me to push those traumas aside and love myself despite them.

One Friday evening during residency, I had vacation time and surprised my parents by coming home from Philly unannounced. My father was at the local watering hole, Hector's Restaurant, so I dropped in on him and his friends. From the age of ten or twelve I'd spent a good deal of time bellied up to the bar (which Papa built) or at the pinball machines learning about life at Hector's with his crew. Walking through the doors, I was bursting with excitement to see my father and his gang again.

"Hooo, look who's here!" they shouted as I magically appeared in the doorway. The prodigal son had returned.

"How's it going?" one asked.

"Let me buy the doctor a beer," another pronounced.

My father's first words upon my arrival were, "No, I got it." Then he slid a five-dollar bill toward the bartender for my beer.

As the crowd left and I was alone with my father for the first time in a long time, he got sentimental.

"How come you never come home?" he asked.

"Dad, what am I supposed to do? I'm busy," I replied.

"Yeah, but..." he reiterated his point. He didn't use many words.

"You wanted your son to be a doctor," I explained.

"Hell, Jack, I didn't care, as long as you didn't end up in jail," he said.

That was all we could say on the subject. We never showed emotions or talked "like girls" back then. We both knew he missed me and wanted me to be home. Although much of the time in school I thought I was doing it to make my parents proud, my success was almost a disappointment to him in that it took me away from him. I missed him too, but was way too far into my training to turn back. That's just the way it was. *I might be back someday*, I told myself.

My reality was so distorted. At the time, I didn't even realize *I* was the important thing to him, not *what I did*. I should have had more confidence that I was truly valuable. They did *everything* to enable me to see that, but that adopted mindset of abandonment and unworthiness still lurked below the surface. It did seem to demand of me that I work harder, but that often pulled me from ever becoming too close to anyone. I didn't feel like I could fully trust anyone. In my delusion, they all seemed out to get me. I see things much more clearly now.

During this process, I have thought a lot about what it has meant to be both Jack and Dr. Rocco. I've also imagined what it would have been like to be Little Larry as well. I've at times been obsessed over my vanished twin. He would have been interesting to know, but for me it's better to realize that he is dead. Like any death, I had to first mourn but then move on. Mourning is not a step you can skip. Unfortunately, I didn't get that memo or even realize a death had occurred until much later in life. That ghost has haunted me many times over the years.

Since acknowledging his death, however, I feel so much better and feel freer to move on. I understand better what role he played in getting me where I am. In addition, I try to live my life in a way that would honor his memory and his story. I do this simply by understanding him and knowing him somewhat more intimately. I didn't know him at all before but now can emulate some of the potential valuable aspects of his life that never were. It's the best thing we can do for our dead, even when it is a former part of ourselves.

For me it has helped to put that vanished twin into the grave, which meant hearing some uncomfortable details as to why he was deemed unworthy to enjoy his natural life. The closure of anyone's death is important, but the demise of my vanished twin has been especially important. He was a huge and irreplaceable part of who I was and am. It is like the loss of a limb, sight, or sound. Once that box was opened, I needed to know the truth in order to move on and live my best life, somewhat in that soul's honor.

While I grappled with my lost twin, those around me had questions about the man who survived. Over the years, those who learned of my adoption would often ask if I thought my nature or nurture had a bigger influence on my life. There is clearly no one answer for anyone, and obviously both are important. Each will be variably dominant depending on which aspect of a person or moment in time we are discussing.

Early on, I always said obviously my family, culture, and nurture were the most important. That was all I knew. After reuniting with Joyce and discovering Larry, I slowly started seeing the natural contributions. Due to my situation, my nature and nurture were presented to me as two separate realities during different periods of my life. This has allowed me to experience each more independently of the other. As a result, I feel as though I'm able to understand better, or at least differently, what each means. With a good deal of effort, I have been able to slowly recognize and tease out the contributions of both my nature and my nurture. Working with a vast number of people as patients and coworkers in intimate situations during this time has also allowed me to see those natural and cultural features in others.

I have finally come to the conclusion that nurture is "them" and nature is "you." When you are raised by your birth parents, "they" are you. Your nurture is your nature and therefore, any difference between the two is difficult to see. Adoptees have a different view.

My admittedly imperfect understanding of it has evolved, and I now believe that nurture is your environment, structure, training, and moral lessons. It is the law and playing fair. It is rigidity, blending imperceptibly, self-control, and climbing up the corporate ladder or military rank structure. It is order, decorum, marriage, alliances, security, predictability, power, religion, rules, hierarchy, and tradition. It wants you to comply, follow the rules, and not stand out.

Nurture is social strata and harmony and defined by society as goodness. It is demonstrated in good times as celebration and in bad as helping your neighbor, banding together to survive, and leaving no man behind. Both situations show the impact, strength, or intensity of your devotion to the collective.

Nurture is also what you think, say, and do around others and how you show emotion publicly. It is that look to the left or right in deciding what to do and the sense of obligation to attend a particular event. Nurture is supportiveness, peer pressure, pettiness, manipulation, and encouragement to go along with or drive the crowd.

It is feminine, calm, regular, and routine, and absolutely necessary for things to stay stable for a significant period of time. It is the nine noble virtues. It can be boring or routine, but it is safe and a fundamental element of society.

Nature, on the other hand, is your genes, your appearance, aptitudes, and personality. It is what you inherently know but may not recognize as your intuition. It is what you feel, *how* you think, speak, and express yourself, often in private. It is your true unadulterated preferences, uniqueness, biases, and the need to belong yet confidence to go it alone.

It comes out strongest in periods of struggle and is seen as one's true colors. It is an individual's range of expression, which may show features of their ethnic or racial diversity.

Nature is selfish, narcissistic, and includes lying, cheating, breaking rules, and looking out only for those who best represent your needs. It is chaos, emotion, love, sex, competition, hate, spirituality, and subconscious backdoor planning. It is disdain or envy of those better than you and joy in realizing your superiority to others. It is panic, meltdowns, unexplainable outbursts, and guttural rage and the shame that exists after those events.

Nature is masculine, bullying and fear of those different than you and the desire to not be that way. Nature is joy, happiness, evil, and the seven deadly sins. It is coy and fickle and survives, therefore is absolutely necessary before anything else can begin. It is fun and the fundamental element of you.

These two forces of nature and nurture ultimately need each other but sometimes must fight one another as if they don't. Given that I was dominated by nurture and denied my nature, I seem to be able to differentiate between the two when they conflict in my daily interactions. It was initially confusing, but with time and experience I've realized that there does seem to be a daily drift between the two on any given day. At times, I seem to be able to travel between the two, back and forth almost on demand. Understanding the similar and different nuances of other cultures over the years has helped as well.

Recognizing nature and nurture and finally experiencing them both simultaneously, I feel incredibly different. I feel whole and awake. I sense my body and my personality as mine, not as something learned or copied from others. I have a heightened awareness of my thoughts, my level of health and rest. I can see myself as being a separate yet complete part of the whole.

I recognize others and can understand the contributions of their nature and nurture as well. I become less frustrated with the direction of life's winds and can more often step back, breathe, re-evaluate, and decide on a different course. I get less upset with the nature or nurture of others when it conflicts with my own. I can appreciate the line of division between my nature and nurture and consciously move between the two depending on the situation. I have learned to say no and can explain why or decide not to explain without offending. That is my free will.

Free will seems to be the wisdom that keeps nature and nurture in check. Free will is your conscience in moderating those two forces. It is your governor, your path. It flows between nature and nurture, depending upon the situation, and is flexible. It is neutral as it mediates, explains, teaches, and tries to understand. It is balance on the spectrum between reckless abandonment and succumbing to control and oppression.

Free will plans your emotions, words, and actions. It evaluates the situation before choosing a reaction. It tells you what you can afford, who you should associate with, and when to call it a day. It tells you when it's best to be emotional and when to rely on your training. It reviews stalemates, arbitrates, and keeps things moving forward or consciously stalls with a purpose. It varies day to day, and is that inner voice which says you've gone too far or not far enough.

Free will maintains harmony, interprets the rules, lobbies for change, and tries to improve the system. It is common sense, bending the rules, forgiving your enemies, and understanding this is not a perfect world.

Maybe it is similar to the Chinese Dao or Tao, "the way." It is that fine invisible line between the sharp contrasts on the yinyang symbol. It is always present but is best witnessed as a meandering path with a wide range of choices on the nature/nurture spectrum. Similarly, in cross section, free will always separates a mix of good/bad, black/white, masculine/feminine, it is never purely either/or but always a combination.

Free will has no gender, doesn't judge, apologizes, and keeps the peace. It is your mirror in that it takes what you see and chooses to construct your reflection into what you want to see.

In trying to reconcile my identity, I've spent a good deal of time during this process staring into the mirror. Regardless of the multiple images I see staring back at me, I realize that, as Jay's mother said, I am who I am. I also have an overwhelming sense of gratitude. I am grateful for the joy and elation as well as the pain and struggles. I love the memories of the ups and downs equally. I cherish the moments where I've exceeded my expectations and also the horrible disappointments that defined my limitations.

In one of his famous works, Nietzsche asked, "What, if some day or night a demon were to steal after you into your loneliest loneliness and say to you: 'This life as you now live it and have lived it, you will have to live once more and innumerable times more; and there will be nothing new in it, but every pain and every joy and every thought and sigh and everything unutterably small or great in your life will have to return to you, all in the same succession and sequence—even this spider and this moonlight between the trees, and even this moment and I myself. The eternal hourglass of existence is turned upside down again and again, and you with it, speck of dust!'"

If I were to be visited by such a devil in the night, I have no doubt that I would answer him clearly and affirmatively with a resounding, "Hell, yeah!" And if I had total awareness, it is my free will to look forward to each day as it unfolds over and over again, the good and the bad.

My grandparents' home was sold soon after they passed away and it took me years before I would even drive by. It was too sad for me to look at it, knowing that they weren't living there anymore. That's gotten better but I still can't get over the fact that my grandfather's trees have all been cut down. I can sometimes muster a drive or walk by the home and thoroughly enjoy the memories as they flood my brain. I like it even better if my kids are with me and I can tell a story or two.

With minimal effort, as I go by I can still see Grama and Papa sitting on the porch. I can smell and taste Gram's ravioli at Christmas dinner. I can hear our voices screaming in the backyard, *"Ghost in the graveyard!"* I can see Aunt B climbing up the stairs while holding onto the railing or someone's arm "just in case." I can hear the men talking shit standing next to the grill and I can hear Aunt Jill saying "Wheee!" because she's worried we're all going to hell. She's in heaven now with Uncle Joe, Aunt B, Grama, and Papa.

Nothing has really changed that much around that two-block radius of 1710 West 24th Street, but for me everything is different. The fog around the whole town and myself seems to have lifted and I can see it all so much clearer. It wasn't ever as perfect as I remember, or rather, everything was perfect just as it was. Even the shitty stuff we tried so hard to bury in the ground with our pears, sticks, and stones was perfect and made us all better, or at least unique. Our desire to keep those evil things from getting us was all in vain, as they eventually worked their way out. We should have just let them be instead of trying to control everything and make the world perfect. I am not so sure what this concept of perfection even is anymore, but I shiver to think that if it weren't for all those shitty things, I wouldn't have had the chance to live such a fantastic life.

Even though I never had a mirror to look into that showed my true reflection, I had plenty of other great mirrors to look into. Here's what I saw in my imperfect mirrors: I saw a family who laughed at, fought with, and loved on each other while simultaneously working their asses off or partying like rock stars every single day in various measure. We were all misfit toys in our own little way and we made fun of everyone equally. We had to make each other tough so no one else's barbs could ever pierce our own thick nurtured skin. You couldn't go outside and let anyone see you had feelings in Erie, Pennsylvania, circa 1970. I could pick on Lisa all day long—and vice versa—but no one else in the world was entitled to touch either of us. In our neighborhood, feelings were something only priests and rich people were allowed to have in public. We didn't know any rich people. If we showed feelings or signs of weakness, they would immediately be jumped on and poked at. We walked out of the house every day with pride and toughness. In the house it was always warm and comforting. Despite the secrets, I was fortunate to be included in that.

I realize now that I was never the prince. I just happened to be someone who they decided to love even if that meant covering up the parts they knew society wasn't prepared to love about me at the time. I'm sad I wasn't a "real Rocco" but I can't tell you how fortunate I was to have been a part of it. I was really just happy to be here and it was all worth it.

I can understand my family much better now and realize that they weren't perfect, but their intentions weren't malicious either. They were just trying to keep their heads down and slide under the radar. All of my extended family and most of the people I knew seemed to be doing the same. We were all more like pawns in acting out society's beliefs and standards at the time and floating down the same river as everyone else.

I have gratitude for the opportunities I've had to laugh and cry, fight with, or love another. I appreciate the moments when I have sought solo space. I am grateful for understanding good intentions and helping others. I've enjoyed the selfishness and satisfaction of fulfilling deep human desires. I am grateful for understanding how I can choose which side of the wall is best for me or my family even when that "best thing" is to *not* be a part of their daily lives. When those times together do occur, I can choose to be a positive part of their lives, not a negative one. I am grateful for being able to fail or disappoint and not beat myself up over it; grateful for being able to better understand myself and what it is to be human. I am still grateful for everything I've experienced.

I may not have been a prince, but I've been a son, a brother, a cousin, a nephew, and a grandson. I've been a Democrat, a Catholic, and a Yankees fan. I've been a husband, a father, a major, a doctor, a success, and a failure. I've been allowed to pretend to be Italian, white, Black, and even immerse myself in an Asian culture for a while, yet was never fully any of the above. I've been relinquished and chosen, abandoned and special. I've been a tragic mistake and a wonderful blessing to so many people. Either way, I had a chance to do it. I am still and always will be grateful for having been recycled, but in the end I'm probably at my best just being me.

AFTERWORD

I originally wrote *Recycled* primarily as my own therapy. The pandemic gave me plenty of time to finally reflect and dig into the adoption issues that I have had my whole life. As the book evolved, I realized I was not alone — among adoptees but also among many individuals trying to battle pathologic nurturing to find their authentic natural self. I think *Recycled* gives a first-hand account of the effects of adoption on the child that is rarely considered.

The 2022 repeal of the Roe v. Wade decision has thrown open the doors to the possible increased use of domestic adoption to counter the expected rise in unwanted pregnancies and births as a result. Opposing groups have made their arguments for and against abortion and adoption but very rarely has the experience of the adoptee been taken into consideration. Often adoptees are used as pawns to support or refute each sides argument. Psychology is rarely this simple. The emotions and thoughts are wide and deep in complexity. Adoptees around the country have an intimate knowledge of the problems with the system and should be included in the discussions.

As a physician I feel a societal responsibility to bring these issues to the public's attention.

———

Beginning with the post WWII baby boom and lasting into the seventies, the Baby Scoop Era, as it has been called, is the United States' most recent experience with wide spread domestic adoption. During this period approximately 4 million children were relinquished by their birth mothers into the hands of agencies and church groups for placement into a more "suitable" family. Two million of these adoptions occurred in the 1960s alone.

Many of the same forces that led to an increase in childbirths during the Baby Boom era also contributed to the rise in pregnancies among unmarried women at that time. A rising economy, increasing freedom among the youth, limited formal sexual education and severely restricted access to birth control saw a rise in unwed births from seven to twenty-three per 1,000. Abortion was illegal, but could still be obtained by any number of back alley clinics — sometimes with severe complications to the mother. For those for whom a shotgun marriage wasn't a viable option, and raising a child on their own deemed social suicide, adoption became the path for many of these *unwanted* children.

For the majority of pregnant women who chose adoption, they often "went away to visit and Aunt" where they found themselves in a maternity home (Home for wayward mothers). While living in these homes prior to their delivery, the women were often asked to think about all the ways this child would be taken better care of by a more decent family. Infertile couples around the country gladly welcomed these unwanted children as a solution to filling their needs for the perfect American family complete with children of their own. The unwed pregnant mother could relinquish her baby, the deserving family could get their child and the infant would be provided a good home in which to be raised. It was presented as the best option for everyone involved.

In retrospect, the abuse of this arrangement is well documented. Georgia Tann's thirty year history of "black market" adoptions in Memphis Tennessee is one of the most commonly cited examples of mass child trafficking during this era. Mothers were coerced to give up their unwanted children and sold to hopeful parents without information and the child's heritage or medical history was lost forever. Adoptive parents were also often not aware of the situation of the birth mother or child.

Catholic Charities and Florence Crittenton Homes among others were frequently involved in the process of receiving unwed women soon after they discovered they were pregnant, preparing them for the relinquishment of the child and then sent back home under a cloak of secrecy so no one would know the ordeal they had just been through. Ann Fessler wrote an incredible account of the experience of many of these birth mothers during this era in her book "The Girls Who Went Away." Fessler summarizes the myriad of examples from increased teenage freedom with automobiles to lack of sexual education and the unavailability of contraception as some of the many reasons for the increase in unwanted pregnancies. Parents, physicians, and clergy members typically encouraged these women into relinquishing their children for adoption. The rationale was that these children could be more properly cared for by more deserving and proper families where they could be raised better.

Nancy Verrier is well respected in the adoption community for her book The Primal Wound about the impact that maternal separation has on the newborn infant. The child has been subconsciously bonding with their mother for nine months and quickly separated from their mother and often sent on a journey of multiple care takers and foster homes until that hopeful day when they will hopefully be brought into this theoretical "better family." Sometimes it works, sometimes it doesn't.

The 2018 documentary Three Identical Strangers highlights the story of identical triplets who were given to three separate families for adoption only to meet and reunite when two were enrolled at the same college. While initially and apparently well adjusted, the separation from their mother, reunion and media frenzy around the event led to a myriad of mental health issues including suicide.

The mystique of the orphan is ubiquitous throughout media and the entertainment industry on a spectrum from Moses and Superman, to Ted Bundy and David Berkowitz, the Son of Sam. Steve Jobs is another well-known adoptee famous for both his meteoric successes with Apple to his notoriously cutthroat and vicious manner in which he dealt with his company and co-workers. The psychological impact of early maternal separation has only partially or superficially been evaluated. Most studies fail to follow these children beyond a few years but we are finding many adoptees continuing to seek mental health support and battling addictions of all sorts at a much higher rate than the general population.

What truly goes on in the mind of an adoptee? The range is wide and varied but there are several common threads which are being discovered and talked about among the very adoptees who are now in their adult years and sharing their stories on social media.

While the two broad categories of hyper-assimilators and rebel adoptee differ on the effect adoption has had on their lives they will often agree on the source of their underlying issues. A sense of abandonment, loss of control, sense of being the outsider and difficulties with relationships, often lead to problems with identity, substance abuse and mental health diagnoses. Suicide is cited as being four times higher among the adoptee community and they receive mental health treatment more than six times the general public.

Many people are amazed with my story and honestly but humbly, so am I. As a physician, it would appear as if I weathered the adoption phenomenon with ease and have become a success in society. Despite that, when I open up to my closest friends or family, they are in disbelief that I would be so insecure. In exploring the subject in depth I'm also surprised that it affected me so much and in so many ways. I drank the Kool-Aid and sang the praises of adoption and my family only to be let down when its effects started undermining the basic foundation of my identity. It wasn't until the collapse that I realized none of that was ever really my natural identity in the first place. My identity was stolen at birth and replaced with a much more *acceptable* identity. The underlying and subconscious effects of the maternal relinquishment are significant, and the fact that a child cannot verbalize or express the resulting emotions should not be misconstrued as a lack of impact. This severe trauma is often sugar coated as a "wonderful thing" for both child and new parents. It is just not true. There are many unintended consequences of both the birth separation and the roses view of the adoption. That initial abandonment has without question dramatically effected my relationships and professional life in many unexpected ways.

Adoption has been at the center of my entire life, both good and bad, and *Recycled* is an honest attempt to look at the issue through the lens that it represented in my life. If it can be of benefit to others going through the journey, I will be happy. If it helps someone else look at adoption in a different way that they haven't considered, I will be proud. Criticism will of course be abundant for every stupid statement I have or will make on the subject. No one is all knowing and I have made many mistakes and I recognize that, as well.

I am not trying to be political but there will be political division on the journey that I have taken. I'm also not trying to be emotional but of course this memoir is my account so it will be emotional to me and my family. I'm not trying to assess the economic impact of the law but there will be impact. This book is quite simply my story and the manner in which I arrived at my current thoughts. This book is an evolution, the same way my knowledge of my self has been and will continue to be an evolution.

We just need to evaluate the impact of early maternal abandonment on the newborn child.

It is not insignificant.

ABOUT THE AUTHOR

An Air Force veteran and orthopedic surgeon, Dr. Rocco has an established practice in Charlotte, N.C. He has chartered medical missions to Madagascar with Operation Small Steps. He's the proud father of two. *Recycled* is his first book.

CPSIA information can be obtained
at www.ICGtesting.com
Printed in the USA
BVHW041933220523
664659BV00001B/1

9 781990 688133